The VOICE of an AFRICAN MAN

calling in the midst of nowhere

Dr Owen OL Black

The VOICE of an AFRICAN MAN

calling in the midst of nowhere

South Africa needs a sound government
that administers a fair regime to her citizens
and every African living under her umbrella
irrespective of colour language or culture

Dr Owen OL Black

Copyright

Copyright by Dr Owen OL Black 2024 ©

The Voice of an Afrcan Man
calling in the midst of nowhere ©

Published by
Dr Owen OL Black

Contact
Dr Owen OL Black
oluhirika@yahoo.com

Edited by
Diane Thompson
di2thomps@gmail.com

DTP
Clive Thompson
International Professional Book Designer
www.getclive.com
email: cliveleet1@gmail.com
+27 83 761 0698 cell

Dedication

My dedication goes to you, my readers

My dedication goes to all my readers – my gratitude to millions of those who choose to read my book around the world.

To my precious family – my wife, *Rosemary Nompumelelo,* and my five wonderful children.

Thank you all for your support during my writing of this book.

Contents

Chapter 1   26
Why an African seeks asylum in his own land

Chapter 2   43
The consideration given in exile

Chapter 3   55
Consideration in the marital perspective

Chapter 4   62
The pressure of life in exile

Chapter 5   74
Accessibility in exile and motive

Chapter 6   83
Mutual love toward immigrants

Chapter 7   91
How to endure in exile

Acknowledgements

Rosemary Nompumelelo,
Appreciation to my wife Rosemary Nompumelelo.

Antonio Damato
My executive secretary Antonio Damato and for the guidelines he gave me.

Dominique
For the typing of this manuscript.

Dr Jacques H Dunia
For contributing many views on the content of this book.

Diane Thompson
Editor Diane Thompson – for the constant way in which she checked every aspect of the content with me.

Clive Thompson
Clive Thompson – for the excellent cover design and the outstanding layout of this book. This is someone you need in your corner!

About the Author

Dr Owen OL Black is originally a Congolese living in South Africa for over two decades and is married to Rosemary Nompumelelo. Dr Owen Luhirika is the author of *The Voice of an African Man calling in the midst of nowhere.*

Dr Owen holds a position of Professor and President at MTBU (Maarifa Theological Bible University. With regard to His academic journey, Dr Owen completed his Bachelor's Degree to Master's degree in Psychology. He then focused on Religious Studies and Theology at the University of KwaZulu-Natal. Both Pietermaritzburg and KZN. This was after completing his Diploma of Theology at Life Center International Bible College, and then continued to further his Religious Studies elsewhere. Pursuing Theology courses, he later completed another Masters of Philosophy and finally obtained his PhD of Philosophy in Florida, Orlando, in the USA. He is now a Senior Professor at Maarifa Theological Bible University.

Dr Owen is an active member of Pan-Africanism. He then obtained an award for Africa Mentorship at PLO Lumumba Foundation In 2020.He also holds an Apostolic office, at the same time, a founder of PGWRC (Power of God's Word Revelation Church) for over a decade in Durban, South Africa.

As this is my first book, I believe it will inspire many, many readers.

Overview

*T*he *Voice of an African Man calling in the midst of nowhere* is a reflection of the experience derived from daily life. I've gained living in SA, being found far from my own maternal home. It is such a big step that one could take to be totally dependent on oneself. Parental orientation is the way out for Africans, it's within African rite of passage, it becomes difficult to depart far from parental care and suddenly become parents yourself. At this point, there is no compromise other than facing reality. There have been few comments and concerns due to the narrative of this book.

Some of my colleagues and I have reflected on this point and happened to be in the same shoes for two and a half decades but some are still found be in a position whereby they can't provide proper documents that allow them to share their experiences with others due to limitations. A big number of Africans run away from facing the fact of African narrative, knowing the truth what will make many to realize that we were all one people, divided by the Western through their gains. It is not easy to narrate the story of our origin to some South Africans that they originate from Central Africa (Congo) some find it as an insult. But the truth is that every African should come to know the history of our Mother Land, that is within the process of psychological liberation.

I've highlighted numbers of issues that limit most of Africans who migrate from one country to another, could this not be the issue between Africans? I am focusing mostly on restrategising the aspect of *Ubuntu* within Africa. The Bantu people are diverse and form a large group of indigenous African ethnic groups who speak Bantu languages. These languages are part of the larger Niger-Congo language family. The Bantu people inhabit a vast region stretching across Central Africa, Southern Africa, and parts of Eastern Africa. They are known for their significant historical migrations, cultural and linguistic diversity, and contributions to the cultural and social landscapes of the African continent.

Historical Migration:
The Bantu expansion is one of the most significant migrations in human history. It began around 2000-3000 BCE from the region of West-Central Africa, near what is now Cameroon and Nigeria. Over several millennia, Bantu-speaking populations gradually spread across sub-Saharan Africa, moving both southwards and eastwards, reaching as far as present-day South Africa and Kenya.

Language:
Bantu languages form one of the largest language families in the world, with over 500 distinct languages and numerous dialects. Some of the most widely spoken Bantu languages include Swahili, Zulu, Xhosa, and Shona. Swahili, in particular, has become a *lingua franca* in many parts of Eastern Africa, including countries like Kenya, Tanzania, and Uganda.

Cultural Diversity:
Despite their shared linguistic roots, Bantu people display a wide range of cultural practices, traditions, and social structures.

Key aspects of many Bantu societies include
Agriculture:
Bantu people traditionally engage in agriculture, cultivating staple crops such as millet, sorghum, maize, and yams. They also practice livestock herding.

Ironworking:
Bantu speakers were early adopters and innovators in iron

smelting and ironworking technologies, which were critical for agricultural tools and weapons.

Social Organization:
Social structures amongst Bantu people can vary widely but often include village-based communities led by a chief or council of elders.

Rituals and Beliefs:
Many Bantu cultures have rich traditions in music, dance, and storytelling. They often practice ancestral worship and have various religious beliefs that include local deities and spirits.

Major Bantu Groups and Regions
West-Central Africa:
Groups such as the Kikongo, Luba, and Kuba inhabit regions in the Democratic Republic of Congo and surrounding areas.

East Africa:
The Kikuyu, Swahili, and Baganda are prominent in countries like Kenya, Tanzania, and Uganda.

Southern Africa:
The Zulu, Xhosa, Shona, and Tswana are among the major Bantu-speaking groups in South Africa, Zimbabwe, Botswana, and Namibia.

Influence and Legacy:
The Bantu expansion not only shaped the demographic and linguistic landscape of Africa but also facilitated the spread of technologies, agricultural practices, and cultural practices. The movement of Bantu-speaking groups led to a rich tapestry of interconnected societies across a vast region.

Contemporary Issues:
Today, the Bantu people face various challenges, including

modernization pressures, land rights issues, and political marginalization in some regions. However, they continue to preserve their languages and cultural heritage while contributing to the contemporary social, political, and economic life of their respective countries.

Overall, the Bantu people and their languages form a significant and influential part of Africa's history and cultural diversity. Irrespective of race or culture, Africa contains a rainbow nation. The diversity should not hinder Africa in enhancing a quality of leadership. Anyone who lives in the land should be able to promote unity in every sector.

Comment

Greetings Dr Owen OL Black.

This book seems to touch some issues which have currently messed up the welfare of Africa. Of course, these are the issues which most immigrants are facing, particularly seeking asylum in their own land! I'm glad you have touched on some of these drawbacks.

What actually is highlighted in this book are the cause factors of xenophobic behaviour that most immigrants undergo. I believe this book will touch millions of people. In addition to this, I can also state that the failure of leadership in Africa goes with the pressure they are experiencing from the West.

There is absolutely nothing that African leaders can do on their own. Some of these leaders have had this misconception wherein they think they can stand alone without help. Therefore, failure in this regard – and with their attitude – will still show up to create more problems.

Thank you for this initiative.
Shout it out, Professor Owen

Dr Muhindo Biryage.

Preface

Adream for every African man will come true when the land embraces total, psychological, economic, political and socio-liberation. Other than these, Africa continues to languish in poverty that is seen as a lake of irrationality.

Africa carries lot of titles which raise so many questions regarding her natural resources. However, the population remains downgradient due to inability to produce thinkers who could be able to lead Africa to take Africa to the next dimension, our African leaders are closing a blind eye toward the issues that hook the land. Rather they embrace their irrelevant leadership making tours abroad while there is so much to fix in their countries.

Addressing these issues that affect Africa in a negative way goes hand in hand with the experience I've gained after many years of learning why African people are suffering from poverty, and yet there is a tremendous richness in the bosom of the land. On the other hand, there is adequate education in Africa, but her people are languished in poverty of mind. Our riches should benefit the people. Let me narrate a beat how rich Africa is, with regard to natural resources.

Africa is endowed with a wealth of natural resources that have significant economic, social, and environmental impacts.

These resources include minerals, fossil fuels, agricultural products, forestry, and freshwater resources. Here's an overview of some of the most prominent natural resources on the continent:

Mineral Resources:
Africa is rich in mineral resources, which have been a major

driver of its economic development. Some key minerals include:

Gold:
Major producers include South Africa, Ghana, and Mali.

Diamonds:
Significant deposits are found in Botswana, South Africa, and the Democratic Republic of Congo (DRC).

Platinum and Palladium:
South Africa is the world's leading producer, accounting for a significant portion of global supplies.

Copper:
Zambia and the DRC are major copper-producing countries.

Cobalt:
The DRC holds over half of the world's cobalt reserves, crucial for rechargeable battery production.

Iron Ore:
Key producers include South Africa, Mauritania, and Liberia.

Bauxite:
Guinea has some of the world's largest bauxite reserves, essential for aluminium production.

Fossil Fuels:
Africa's fossil fuel resources are crucial for both the continent and the global energy market.

Oil:
Nigeria, Angola, and Libya are among Africa's top oil producers. The continent has significant oil reserves, particularly in the Gulf of Guinea and North Africa.

Natural Gas:
Major reserves are found in Algeria, Nigeria, Egypt, and

Mozambique. Recent discoveries have increased interest in East Africa's gas potential.

Coal:
South Africa has the largest coal reserves in Africa, used predominantly for electricity generation and export.

Agricultural Resources:
Africa's diverse climates and fertile soils support a wide range of agricultural products:

Cash Crops:
Cocoa (Ivory Coast, Ghana), coffee (Ethiopia, Uganda), tea (Kenya), and cotton (Mali, Burkina Faso).

Staple Crops:
Maize, millet, sorghum, and cassava, which are essential for food security across the continent.

Horticulture:
Fruits and vegetables, including bananas, citrus fruits, and flowers, especially in countries like Kenya and South Africa.

Forestry Resources:
Africa's forests provide timber, fuelwood, and other non-timber forest products. Key forest regions include:

The Congo Basin:
The second-largest tropical rainforest in the world, spanning six countries and providing a critical habitat for biodiversity.

West African Rainforests:
These forests have been heavily impacted by deforestation but still provide timber and other resources.

Miombo Woodlands:
Stretching across several Southern African countries, these woodlands supply fuelwood, charcoal, and medicinal plants.

Freshwater Resources:
Africa is home to major rivers, lakes, and aquifers that are vital for drinking water, agriculture, and hydropower:

River Systems:
The Nile, Congo, Niger, and Zambezi rivers are among the most significant.

Lakes:
Major lakes include Lake Victoria, Lake Tanganyika, and Lake Malawi.

Aquifers:
Large groundwater reservoirs such as the Nubian Sandstone Aquifer System provide critical water supplies to arid regions.

Challenges and Opportunities

Sustainability and Environmental Impact:
Overexploitation, deforestation, and climate change pose significant threats to Africa's natural resources. Sustainable management practices are crucial for preserving these resources for future generations.

Economic Development:
While rich in resources, many African countries face challenges such as inadequate infrastructure, political instability, and governance issues, which can impede the equitable and effective use of these resources.

Global Market Fluctuations:
The economies of many African countries heavily dependent on commodity exports can be vulnerable to global market volatility.

Technological Advancements:
Emerging technologies and better resource management practices offer opportunities to maximize the benefits derived from Africa's natural resources while minimizing

environmental and social impacts.

Africa's wealth of natural resources offers significant potential for boosting economic development, improving livelihoods, and fostering sustainable development. However, realizing this potential requires addressing the myriad challenges associated with resource management, governance, and environmental conservation.

Introduction

Dear readers

Exile is a state of being forced to live away from one's home country or community due to political, social or personal reasons. People may be exiled for a variety of reasons, including persecution, political unrest, conflict or seeking better opportunities abroad. Life in exile can be challenging and often involves coping with feelings of loss, isolation and uncertainty about the future. For many individuals, exile means leaving behind their families, friends and familiar surroundings, leading to a sense of disconnection and longing for home. Adjusting to a new culture, language and way of life can be difficult and feelings of loneliness and alienation are common among exiles.

Exiles often face practical challenges as well, such as finding employment, housing, and access to essential services in a new country. Legal and bureaucratic hurdles may also complicate their situation, as exiles may struggle to secure residency or refugee status, leaving them in a state of limbo.

Despite the hardships, many exiles display resilience, strength and a determination to make a new life for themselves in their adopted country. They may form tight-knit communities with other exiles, providing mutual support and solidarity in the face of adversity.

Overall, life in exile can be a complex and emotional experience, marked by a constant negotiation of identity, belonging and survival in unfamiliar surroundings. It often involves a mix of challenges and opportunities as exiles navigate the complexities of starting anew while holding onto their memories and connections to their homeland.

The pontification of exile refers to the idea of assigning a specific purpose or reason to someone's experience of being in exile. This can involve viewing exile as a form of punishment, a means of political suppression or a necessary sacrifice for the greater good. The pontification of exile can also involve ascribing positive aspects to the experience such as personal growth, resilience or the opportunity for a fresh start in a new environment.

From a political perspective, the pontification of exile may be used by governments or authorities to justify their actions in forcing individuals to leave their home country. By framing exile as a necessary measure to maintain stability or national security, those in power may seek to downplay the hardships and injustices faced by exiles.

On the other hand, exiles themselves may also find meaning in their experience by attributing a specific purpose or goal to their displacement. This could involve seeing exile as an opportunity for personal growth, a chance to advocate for political change or a way to build connections and solidarity with other marginalised communities.

Overall, the pontification of exile is a complex and often contested concept that reflects the diverse ways in which individuals and societies interpret and make sense of the experience of being in exile. It can involve both positive and negative interpretations, highlighting the multidimensional nature of exile and its impact on individuals and communities.

Prologue

African leaders are failing to lead effectively and address pressing issues in their countries. Some leaders are more focused on personal gain and power struggles, rather than the wellbeing of their citizens. Corruption is rampant, resources are mismanaged and human rights abuse. The grass roots are ignored. These failures have led to widespread of poverty, inequality and political instability across the continent. African leaders must prioritise the needs of their people and work towards sustainable development and progress for all.

Why doesn't Africa have something she owns?

Africa does have a lot of natural resources and attributes that are unique to the continent, including diverse cultures, rich natural resources as mentioned above, beautiful landscapes and a deep sense of community. However, historical and ongoing challenges such as colonisation, exploitation, political instability and corruption have hindered Africa's ability to fully harness its potential and develop its own industries, technologies and innovations.

Additionally, the global economic system has often favoured more developed countries, making it difficult for African nations to compete on an equal playing field. Without adequate infrastructure, education and support systems in place, African countries have struggled to fully capitalise on their own resources and capabilities.

There have been efforts in recent years to promote African entrepreneurship, innovation and self-reliance. However, there is still a long way to go in terms of empowering African countries to fully leverage their own strengths and opportunities. Empowering and supporting African leaders and entrepreneurs, investing in education and infrastructure and promoting fair trade and partnerships are all essential steps in helping Africa realise its full potential and build a brighter future for its people.

Where did we go wrong?

These issues facing Africa today can be traced back to a combination of historical factors including colonisation, exploitation and the legacy of slavery. European colonial powers carved up the continent without regard for ethnic or cultural boundaries, leading to the creation of artificial nation-states that often lacked cohesion and unity. This legacy of colonialism left African countries with fragile institutions, unequal distribution of resources and a deep-rooted culture of corruption and nepotism.

Following independence, many African nations struggled with political instability, dictatorships and civil wars as leaders vied for power and resources. Foreign intervention and exploitation further destabilised the region, with Western powers often supporting corrupt or authoritarian regimes in exchange for access to natural resources.

Additionally, the lack of investment in education, infrastructure and healthcare has hindered the development of African economies and limited opportunities for growth and progress. The debt burden imposed by international lenders has also hampered economic development and perpetuated a cycle of dependency.

Moving forward, it is essential for African leaders to prioritise good governance, accountability and sustainable development in order to overcome these historical challenges and build a more prosperous and equitable future for the continent. Investment in education, infrastructure and healthcare, as well as promoting fair trade and partnerships, will be crucial to unlocking Africa's full potential and addressing the root causes of poverty and inequality.

Economical deficit in Africa.

The economic deficits in many African countries can be attributed to a variety of factors including poor governance, corruption, mismanagement of resources, lack of investment in key sectors and political instability. African leaders have often prioritised their own interests over those of the country, leading to widespread corruption and embezzlement of public funds. This has contributed to a lack of accountability and transparency in government, hindering economic progress and development.

Mismanagement of natural resources, particularly in natural resource-rich countries, has also been a significant issue. Many African countries have struggled to effectively negotiate fair deals with international corporations, leading to exploitation of resources without adequate benefit to the local population. The lack of diversification in economies, overreliance on a few key industries and weak regulatory frameworks have further exacerbated economic deficits in the region.

Political instability, conflict and governance challenges have also had a detrimental impact on economic growth in many African countries. Insecurity and instability deter investment, disrupt trade and hinder development efforts. Lack of investment in crucial sectors such as education, healthcare and infrastructure has limited the ability of African countries to build a strong and sustainable economy.

Overall, African leadership must prioritise good governance, transparency, accountability and the rule of law in order to address economic deficits and create an environment conducive to sustainable economic growth and development. Investment in key sectors, promotion of entrepreneurship and innovation and fostering a business-friendly environment are all essential steps in overcoming the economic challenges facing many African countries.

Something needs to be done. An African man cannot state that Africa is the continent full of abundance because these things somehow sound like a fairy tale.

Chapter 1

Why an African man seeks asylum in his own land

This is a unique chapter where I'm basically explaining about the experiences I've gained over the years of my staying in SA. As the author of this book, I would like to raise certain points about the land of Africa and her endowment, when we talk of this land, we are bringing *Mama* Africa's beauty to be known, thus there are millions of Africans who do not know the goodness of *Mama* Africa yet they live the continent of Africa. Called sons and Daughters of *Mama* Africa. i.e. Every region of *Mama* Africa should be able to promote stability and welfare to those that are willing to repatriate back to the Mother Land. We need to involve our brothers and sister who long went into slavery that are found across Europe, America etc. those who would like to come back, ought not to be questioned or hindered to come back home. They need to be treated well and be hospitable to the diaspora, and welcome them back to their roots.

As for the Africans living in the land, they must consider one another with respect and love due to sharing some resources that are found throughout the continent.

There are many questions you may ask yourself which may make you freak out, especially when life turns one into an asylum seeker in this land. How can this be explained to a person who knows that he belongs to the land? How can an African man become an asylum seeker in his own land? These are questions that probe people's minds from time to time. When trying to figure out whether we are strangers in our own land, who if we are autochthons (an original or indigenous inhabitant of a place), should be given consideration that will allow us to claim the rights of a citizenship of Africa. In this alone, I have raised so many questions that will help those who are found living in SA. And to urge them to understand the failure of African people, it is not caused by our forefathers or exonerate for a fault of their lowliness of not willing to implement the right means to save Africa. It is within a failing to find leaders that are nationalist and able to fit into leadership that we want. I have again highlighted the ignorance of some leaders. They become so blasé that they forget Africa has its own people. Many times, we find that Africans are refugee in their own Land. But this does not apply to our younger brothers who will never come to Africa, and remain a refugee, or become one. There is always consideration given to them, a special treatment for that case.

We somehow wonder why things are done this way? Then we look at what transpired in Africa that raises our attention more and more. Many may not say anything about it. They may be silent or late make noise about it. It is time to break from psychological limitation between Africans. It's time to break free from the limitations from imperialism.

The time has arrived to break free from psychological limitations of colonialism, whether you disagree with me or not, but we are still colonised indirectly by a system set to systemize our moves, doing, thinking etc. there are three major systems: including education, religion, as well as western law that makes every African guilty of all atrocity that is intolerable. That's why they set laws that contain traps to make some African brothers vulnerable in any situation. Actually, as an African, it is your right to know that you have to stand by your rights and for the truth. As spoken in the Holy Bible, *only the truth can set us free.*

The truth is, there are a lot of things still hidden concerning Mother Africa and the wellbeing of Africans themselves. It's been hijacked. As Africans, we need to fix that. It's not good to sit and watch. It's time to emancipate from slavery mentality and bring hope to the broken people for the betterment of Africa's future.

We believe that Africa will be liberated and free from setbacks that was caused by a colonial system, who will continue on what our predecessors started, the giants of peace stood before us, who were trying to bring Africa to its original state. However, many of them are long gone. There are other giants now rising and standing who are trying to bring Africa together within the context of freedom. Many Africans might be scattered even outside Africa, but we are all contributing to uniting Africa and fighting imperialism that has long taken place into African's system of leadership.

Africans will understand that it's time to live free in their own motherland. It is time to stand up and acquire what belongs to us. It is time to stand up and sing a new song – a song of salvation; a song of freedom; a song that will bring joy into the future of our children. It is time for Africa to arise and put on the garments of honour.

- Africa has been mutilated for too long.
- Africa has been denigrated for so long.
- Africa has been under a subject of colonial trades but this is a moment that Africa is going to stand up.
- It is a moment that Africa is going to arise with the power of God.

So, we are going to subdue every enemy that arises against Africa, like we've seen how many have arisen in course of the years gone by, others in the form of sickness and others in the form of change of nature etc. Fighting these things not by violence, but by intellectual means, through intelligence. Notification is how we are going to bring the awareness of freedom to Africans, and the indications are given that were started with our giants of peace – the heroes who held meetings which took place in 1963 in Ethiopia, including Marcus Garvey of Jamaica, Haile Selassie of Ethiopia, Muammar Gaddafi of Libya and Kwame Nkrumah of Ghana.

What was the content about the meeting that took place in Ethiopia in 1963?

The meeting that took place in Ethiopia in 1963 was the founding conference of the Organisation of African Unity (OAU), which was held in Addis Ababa from May 22 to May 25. This historic event brought together representatives from 32 independent African states at the time. The primary goal was to promote unity and solidarity among African countries, facilitate cooperation, and eradicate colonialism and apartheid from the continent.

Key outcomes of the meeting included:

Charter of the Organisation of African Unity:
The representatives adopted the OAU Charter, which outlined the principles and objectives of the organization.

Aimed to Promote Unity:
The meeting underscored the importance of African unity in achieving political, economic, and social progress.

Commitment to Decolonization:
One of the main objectives was to accelerate the decolonization process across the continent and to support liberation movements in the remaining colonized territories.

Non-alignment and Sovereignty:
The African leaders advocated for non-alignment in global politics and a commitment to the sovereignty and territorial

integrity of African states.

Structural Formation:
The conference established several organs of the OAU, including the Assembly of Heads of State and Government, the Council of Ministers, the General Secretariat, and several specialized commissions.

This meeting marked a pivotal moment in African history as it laid the groundwork for greater cooperation and mutual support among African nations, ultimately contributing to the continent's ongoing struggles for independence, unity, and development. The OAU was later replaced by the African Union (AU) in 2002, which continues to work towards many of the original goals set forth in 1963.

There are so many others who support Africa's economical build up, and they are upcoming, like Julius Malema who strongly advocates fairness by fighting corruption and the right of citizens of Africa economically, and currently a dynamic leader of an opposition party called EFF (Economic Freedom Fighters) in SA, who contributed to the betterment of the Africa in general. There are so many who have gone before us too, who seemed to be the voices of Africa. Nevertheless, Africa is raising up new liberators who are playing a crucial role to liberate Africans from psycho-economical slavery. This freedom transpires every time Africans get educated about knowing what causes setbacks throughout the continent. There is a tremendous paradigm shift with regard to educative system, sooner or later, all Africans will join together in love, and understanding their responsibility of what belongs to Africans.

And another Unifier of African Americans Diaspora. Known by the name of Dr Arikana Chihombori from Zimbabwe, a former African Union Secretary.

Others like Prof. PLO Lumumba from the Kenya who

dynamically addresses the issues and errors that Africa needs to be aware of, and rectify them. Africa has another brother called Joshuah Maponga, who plays a crucial role to bring Africa awareness to term. Another is an African Ambassador, Dr Susan Tatah, from Pan-African Daily TV living in Germany.

Another thing, based on condemnation, is that I've been carried into the minds of many Africans for some time. This goes toward the question that has been paused from time to time. And this is the concerns for every immigrant who is found outside his native land, which is; *Why an African seeks asylum in his own land.* That is impossible and unacceptable. It's not something that anyone can understand – like a European seeking asylum in Europe. Obviously, that does not take place only in Africa where Africans have been subjected to so many things that the FDA took a long time to deal with them. Africans have been subjected to humiliation, denigration, confusion and various other forms of abuse.

We and our children are confused. Our children are being born into a confused world due to what is happening in Africa. When we go to certain African countries and to Immigration, we find that many Africans are mutilating other Africans' identities and are trying to oppress them by calling them refugees and other degrading names. This is unacceptable in Africa. All Africans should be able to claim their rights.

Africans should not be regarded as refugees in their own land. There shouldn't be restrictions for Africans, and our identity should be our colour because it is unique. There is originality in the African colour. When God made Africans, it was done with all His heart. That's why the body and system of Africans contains originality. There is nothing fake or counterfeit. All is pure. Africans are made in the image of God.

With this, there's a lot to speak about regarding Africa and its diversity. Africa is a great place to live in. If we are not oppressed with anything that causes discomfort, then growth must take place. Africans should be able to understand that the land of our ancestors needs a breakthrough. The land of a black man is a lens to look through where we should not experience any form of mutilation or violence, or any form of killing and all types of atrocities that are taking in most place today.

Africa is our motherland and we are going to prepare Africa for better things. This book will help the readers to understand the essentials of Africanism, and as you read it, many questions will come to you. There are many things revealed in this book, a lot of it appeared to be historically mentioned. The stereography of this book lies on so many facts and experiences on the readers hereof, will greatly benefit in knowledge otherwise they are with regard things that are still to be concealed.

Africa is our land, our motherland, the land of honey and milk. Africans need to be more courageous in exploiting the land between themselves. Misery has been an ongoing kind of life; marginalization has been a tool used to demoralize her people. Though this road, we have encountered many surprises and challenges over the decades.

I found it very challenging to be alone with no mother or father. I was surrounded by individuals who camouflaged their personalities due to the hardness of life and its monotonous routine. In the year of 2000, I took a trip to one of the African countries – Mozambique.

I found Mozambique a pleasant country with lovely people who were caring and sympathetic. This was a great occasion. The fact that I was welcomed into the country and the generosity received by its citizens was admirable. Sometimes I would take a walk and, while I was among the mass of people, I would marvel at their numbers, being unable to count the multitude of different events around me.

My mind would wander and questions would immerge upon that. I ruminate on these events from time to time. It felt strange which made me ask myself: *"Do all these people know one another?"* Although I knew it was impossible that all these people from different diverse backgrounds could possibly know one another, yet there was a certain occasion which brought them together where they united linguistically and spiritually as though they did know one another.

When this special occasion came to pass, I immediately found the answer to my question which showed me that they had unity among themselves which, in turn, allowed people to speak and think the same. As a leader, I found this to be very poignant. It struck me that all these people could unify in their vast multitude, yet not know one another. Only unity can bring people to such a level of togetherness which is so needed in our world today.

At that point, I could not speak their vernacular, neither understand anything from the Portuguese that was spoken around me.

All I could speak was English, French and a few other African languages. I pondered on this language conundrum as I watched my steps, walking from the hotel room, heading to my chosen destination for something to eat – the marketplace.

Along the way, I came across a gentleman and I tried to engage with him, speaking with him, he then changed my question completely, that I had kept asking myself. This now changed to frustration. If I can remember correctly, my words to him were a simple greeting in English.

My aim was to get further ahead in asking a few questions concerning the destination which I took. It was extremely difficult with the issue of language which I faced. Therefore the gentleman's response bamboozled me completely. I thought that I was going to get help, but instead, he made me realise that language was the problem, and got nowhere.

The fact is, I had little knowledge of the communication barrier found in a foreign country, I felt apprehension well up inside me which couldn't be helped. As I was about to enter the marketplace, I stopped, becoming aware that all the people were obliged to produce their identity cards, myself included. This made me think of my question which came to mind once more as to how all these people from diverse backgrounds and ethnic groups were unknown by one another, yet they were known by the government.

I had found the answer to my question – the diversity of Africa lies within the people that are found in the continent of Africa.

Regarding other diaspora such as Europeans, Asians and Americans, all these people make up the 'Rainbow Nation', including those that are found around the Caribbean. Our rainbow nation is not only seen or verbalised anyhow, it is also the reality we live in that is to be demonstrated by people from different backgrounds. This should not be undermined by any ethnic group or religious party, nevertheless, the facts is facts.

Being a rainbow nation brings different mindsets together with accepting one another's beliefs, cultures, traditions and existence. Accommodating other types of indigenous groups, it strengthens Africa, giving the country a good aspect of becoming champions within the geopolitical market. The dynamism of Africa lies in *'Ubuntu'*, other than that we failing to unite. This is the only thing that can make us strong. If not, Africa will be seen as a weak place with regression and corruption ruling over her natives. But this can take place when Africa stands alone.

Why is it that Africa can't stand alone in terms of finances and development?

The notion that Africa cannot stand alone in terms of finances and development is a complex and multifaceted issue that stems from a combination of historical, political, economic, and social factors. Here are several key reasons:

Historical Legacy of Colonialism:
The colonial history of Africa had long-lasting impacts. European powers exploited African resources and structured the economies of African nations to serve the needs of the colonizers. This exploitation left many African countries with economies heavily dependent on a few commodities and with little industrial infrastructure.

Political Instability:
Post-independence, many African nations have experienced political instability, including coups, civil wars, and authoritarian regimes. This instability often undermines economic development by creating an environment where long-term planning is difficult and investors are wary.

Economic Challenges:
Many African countries struggle with weak financial systems, limited access to capital, and high levels of debt. Additionally, while some African nations are rich in natural resources, they often lack the infrastructure and technology to fully benefit from these resources. In many cases, profits from resource extraction are taken by foreign companies or through corrupt practices.

Healthcare and Education:
Poor healthcare and education systems limit human capital development. High levels of disease, lack of access to quality education, and brain-drain (where educated individuals leave the country) all hinder economic growth and development.

International Trade Dynamics:
The global trade system often disadvantages African countries. Many African nations export raw materials and import finished goods, leading to trade imbalances.

Additionally, tariff and non-tariff barriers, subsidies to farmers in developed countries, and other trade policies can limit the ability of African countries to compete in global markets.

Infrastructure Deficit:
There is a significant infrastructure deficit in many African countries. Poor transportation networks, unreliable electricity supplies, and inadequate water and sanitation systems can make doing business more difficult and expensive.

Dependency on Aid:
Many African countries have become dependent on foreign aid, which can create a cycle of dependency. While aid can provide essential support, it is not always used effectively and can sometimes undermine local governance structures.

Corruption:
Corruption remains a significant issue in many African countries. It diverts resources away from development efforts, undermines trust in institutions, and deters both domestic and international investment.

Global Financial Systems:
The global financial system can also pose challenges. Access to international finance markets can be limited, and fluctuations in global commodity prices can have outsized influences on African economies.

Climate Change and Environmental Challenges

Africa is particularly vulnerable to climate change impacts, such as droughts, floods, and desertification, which can devastate agricultural productivity and displace populations.

That said, it's important to recognize that Africa is incredibly diverse, with 54 countries each having distinct experiences and challenges. There are countries within Africa that have made significant strides in development and finance.

Countries like Rwanda, Botswana, Ghana, and Senegal have seen substantial economic growth and improvements in governance and infrastructure. Sustainable development in Africa will likely require a combination of internal reforms, regional cooperation, and a supportive international environment.

For Africa to stand alone it will need Africans who have understood the European system of which they used to colonize Africa to this far how it works.

The myth history of Africa lies in dreams and visions toward humanity. A prominent religious leader of the epoch, Martin Luther King, stated *"I have a dream"*. That alone brought the mystery of our visions to unfold into the natives of Africa.

Today, we see Africa in a different view, mainly the incorruptible brown Africans 'African Indians', 'African Europeans', 'Asian Africans' etc. Thus, everyone who is born in Africa is automatically African. This gives legitimacy to being an African. Through this concept and paradigm shift, unity will be birthed and natives will easily accept one another without segregation or racial discrimination.

Shortly after the realisation of this concept, I found myself in my hotel room with another fellow – a Chinese immigrant. We shared a common challenge in that we could not understand one another linguistically as well as not knowing our way around the city.

Thus, we were both found to be 'mutes' to one another, and this reminded me of a story in the Holy book which tells a story of the 'Tower of Babel' which was constructed by people who spoke one language who, thereafter, could not understand one another due to the variety of languages which God used to thwart their evil schemes and disperse them throughout the earth. That is how languages emerged – this was the beginning of division here on Earth.

There is a reason why I state that Africa should depend on herself by all means so that she should be able to cater for her rainbow nation.

Your sentiment underscores an essential aspiration for many African countries: achieving greater self-reliance and sustainable development to better cater to the needs of their diverse populations. Here are some key strategies and pathways that can help African nations move toward economic independence and improved welfare for all citizens:

Economic Diversification – Industrial Development:
Investing in manufacturing and processing industries to add value to raw and reduce reliance on commodity exports.

Agricultural Modernization:
Enhancing agricultural productivity through technology, improved practices, and infrastructure to ensure food security and create export opportunities.

Service Sector Expansion:
Promoting sectors such as tourism, finance, and information technology to diversify income sources.

Strengthening Regional Integration AFCFTA (African Continental Free Trade Area):
Leveraging continental trade to build larger, more competitive markets, reduce trade barriers, and foster economic cooperation.

Regional Infrastructure Projects:
Collaborating on cross-border infrastructure projects such as transportation, energy, and communications to facilitate trade and movement.

Building Human Capital:

Education:
Investing in education from primary to higher levels,

emphasizing STEM (Science, Technology, Engineering, and Mathematics) fields to build a skilled workforce.

Healthcare:
Improving healthcare systems to enhance the overall well-being and productivity of the population.

Vocational Training:
Providing vocational and technical training to equip citizens with practical skills for various industries.

Good Governance and Institutional Strengthening

Transparency and Accountability:
Implementing robust anti-corruption measures to ensure that public resources are used effectively.

Effective Public Institutions:
Strengthening institutions to improve service delivery, policy implementation, and economic planning.

Investment in Infrastructure Transportation:
Developing roads, railways, ports, and airports to facilitate movement and trade.

Energy:
Expanding access to reliable and affordable energy sources, including renewable energy, to support industrial and domestic needs.

Technology and Communication:
Investing in ICT infrastructure to support digital economies and innovation.

Fostering Innovation and Entrepreneurship

Tech Hubs and Innovation Centres:
Supporting the development of innovation hubs and incubators to nurture startups and tech enterprises.

Access to Finance:
Ensuring that small and medium-sized enterprises (SMEs) have access to financing options to grow their businesses.

Promoting Sustainable Development

Environmental Protection:
Implementing policies to manage natural resources sustainably and address climate change.

Inclusive Growth:
Ensuring that economic growth benefits all segments of society, reducing inequality and poverty.

Developing Strong Trade Policies

Fair Trade Agreements:
Negotiating trade agreements that benefit African countries and protect their economic interests.

Promoting Exports:
Enhancing the capacity to export higher-value goods and services.

Harnessing Diaspora Resources

Remittances and Investments:
Encouraging the African diaspora to invest in domestic projects and businesses.

Knowledge and Skills Transfer:
Leveraging the expertise and knowledge of the diaspora to fill skills gaps and drive innovation.

Successful Examples

Ethiopia:
Notable for its investments in infrastructure and industrial parks, aiming to become a manufacturing hub.

Rwanda:
Praised for its governance, business-friendly environment, and efforts in ICT development.

Botswana:
Known for prudent management of natural resources and strong governance, contributing to steady economic growth.

Achieving greater economic independence and the capacity to cater to the diverse needs of African societies requires a multifaceted approach, combining economic, social, and political reforms. By focusing on internal strengths, fostering regional cooperation, and pursuing sustainable and inclusive development strategies, African nations can build resilient economies and improve the quality of life for their people. The journey is challenging but not insurmountable, and the progress made so far by various countries is a testament to the potential for transformation and growth.

Thus, when it came to verbal communication between the Chinese brother and me, the results were of nightmarish proportions. Eventually we found a way to communicate with each other effectively. This brought us together to a point of telling each story as if we were both speaking the same language. Thus, we were done using gestures.

This taught me something. In life, we should accommodate people by loving them, even though we can't understand their vernacular. Love motivates us to know about our neighbours or those whom we meet in life, even if we can't understand them through verbal communication. Love in itself is a universally understood language.

What amazed me was that, whenever the Chinese brother and I worked, we were identified by the police and a few other people. The reason for this was that our knowledge about that particular city was very limited and our destination was slightly different even though we'd stayed together for a few days. Before parting, he stated a point which was very crucial.

Although he struggled in expressing himself, the main point I understood was that life outside one's native country is not easy. Even if one is able to express oneself, there are still some problems which can highlight different things such as culture and language, among other aspects. He said again that visitors are exposed to danger because of the inability to distinguish between the right way to one's destination and the wrong way that can potentially be dangerous.

Chapter *2*

The consideration given in exile

Part Two is a presentation of *Chapter Two* of this book. This chapter narrates the pressure experienced on a daily basis, particularly to those living in exile. My focus reflects issues I've encountered that varies to different anomalies looking from past and present experiences. They both reveal a reality known by those who have been in exile and experienced a life similar to this, and probably more.

I also stress other political issues that we've had for the past 60 years which seem to be a stumbling block to the African continent. Some of these issues have rendered misery to Africans, such as socio-economic issues, socio-demographic, socio-political, socio-racist the sociocentric of the book highlights various major points that cannot be ignored. Economy is the key fundamental to leadership and we may inquire or question the following:

How long shall Africa remain a baby economically?

The perception of Africa as 'economically immature' is both complex and misleading. The continent is incredibly diverse, comprising 54 countries, each with its own unique challenges, opportunities, and levels development. Several African nations have made significant strides in economic growth and development over recent decades.

However, there are ongoing challenges that need to be

addressed for sustained and broad-based economic growth across the continent. Here are several key steps and factors that could contribute to economic maturation in Africa:

Political Stability and Good Governance

Transparent and Accountable Institutions:
Strengthening institutions to ensure transparency, accountability, and the rule of law is essential.

Reduction of Corruption:
Efforts to combat corruption will help in better resource allocation and investment confidence.

Economic Diversification

Broadening Economic Base:
Moving beyond dependency on natural resources by diversifying into manufacturing, services, and technology sectors.

Value-Added Processes:
Enhancing capabilities in processing and manufacturing to retain more economic value within the continent.

Infrastructure Development

Investing in Infrastructure:
Building and improving transportation networks, energy infrastructure, and digital connectivity.

Public-Private Partnerships:
Leveraging partnerships to fund and manage large-scale infrastructure projects.

Human Capital Development

Education and Training:
Investing in education systems and vocational training to

build a skilled workforce.

Healthcare Systems:
Strengthening healthcare to improve the overall productivity and well-being of the population.

Financial Systems

Access to Capital:
Developing financial institutions and markets to improve access to credit and investment.

Support for SMEs:
Creating an environment that supports small and medium-sized enterprises, which are often key drivers of economic growth.

Regional Integration and Trade

Intra-African Trade:
Strengthening regional trade agreements and the African Continental Free Trade Area (AfCFTA) to increase trade among African nations.

Global Trade Participation:
Enhancing competitiveness to better participate in global markets.

Technological Innovation

Adoption of Technology:
Embracing digital technologies to leapfrog traditional development stages.

Supporting Startups:
Creating ecosystems that support technological startups and innovation.

Agricultural Development

Modernizing Agriculture:
Investing in modern agricultural practices and technologies to increase productivity and food security.

Rural Development:
Ensuring inclusive development by enhancing infrastructure and services in rural areas.

Sustainable Development

Environmental Sustainability:
Implementing policies that promote sustainable resource use and address climate change.

Inclusive Growth:
Ensuring that economic growth benefits all segments of the population, reducing inequality.

Cultural and Social Factors

Harnessing Demographic Dividend:
Leveraging the young and growing population by investing in youth education and employment opportunities.

Promoting Peace and Security:
Addressing conflicts and ensuring stable, peaceful societies conducive to economic activities.

Progress and Future Prospects

Success Stories:
Countries like Rwanda, Botswana, Kenya, Ghana, and Ethiopia have shown steps towards economic maturity through various reforms and targeted investments.

External Partnerships:
Strategic international partnerships focused on mutual benefits and sustainability can accelerate progress.

While significant work remains, the trajectory towards

economic maturity is within reach for many African nations. The timelines can vary significantly from one country to another based on domestic policies, political will, and global economic conditions. Sustained effort, visionary leadership, and inclusive policies will be crucial in ensuring that Africa's economic potential is fully realized in the coming decades.

The book touches most of the elementary key points that Africa needs to focus on in order to free Africa from the stagnation of illusion.

This book is written by Owen Black I.K., and shares his personal experiences regarding life in exile. This script does not come from other scholars. It cames from what he's been through and what challenged him to the extent of writing concerning life he's experienced daily outside of his native country. This chapter does not only deal with hard times, but also good times, although these haven't been long-lasting. The majority of his experiences were hard times, including deceptions from relationships I encountered through a young girl, was very disappointing to me, but I kept a record of it to help someone who may be going through this in the future.

This girl was 23. She was able to master three older men. The oldest was 63 years of age who was her uncle and boyfriend. The second eldest was 53, with myself as the youngest in my thirties. When she was born, the expenses were paid for by three people and we had no knowledge of one another. Each of us thought the child was our own. The baby was a girl who happened to reveal the secret, at the age of three, when her 'fathers' were introduced to her. She then revealed the truth to me as to who the father was. I remember one day we had a conversation with the child whereby she proved to me that I was not the father. She knew the eldest man as the father but she told me the father lived in the suburb where she was residing.

That was when I decided I needed to know the truth. Henceforth, I was able to know every hidden secret. I had to confront her. Unfortunately, the man, who had also been deceived, arrived. At this point, the armed man knew his intention was to kill me. It was a Wednesday morning around six when I received a phone call. I was asked whether I was the man he was looking for as he had requested to see me. I was working as a receptionist in a hotel at the time. I agreed and, at around eight in the morning, we met. He was unsmiling but, on introduction, he realised I had also been deceived. After some discussion, he informed me that we had both been deceived. He stated that I must thank my God that I was also free as he was well prepared to terminate my life.

He stated that the child did not have any resemblance to me as the child's complexion was very light. He said the complexion didn't match mine and he could see there was no resemblance to me. Thereafter he stated that he wanted me to know the truth. He showed me his pistol, shook my hand and apologised. He said he was going to kill an innocent man who had been deceived in the same way he had been. Due to our similar predicaments, he took me to the workplace of the eldest man. We arrived at a hotel and he called his name.

The man came down but, upon seeing who we were, he fled in anger. That's when I knew I had truly been deceived. I could see the child resembled the sixty-four-year-old. After taking care of the child for three years, this was the end of that relationship filled with lies and illusion. In the same story of life in exile, I've realised that language has a big impact which can assist in the accumulation of knowledge regarding culture in that particular place or country one lives in. I wanted to know the dialect in order to make my journey easier. Every spoken language is easy and a passive means to enable a safe journey to one's chosen destination.

It couldn't be difficult for me to learn, especially when I found other people who were foreigners like me in the country. Therefore, I found it quite interesting to have the basics of the language which made things work for me. I didn't have an alternative. Thus, forcing myself to learn a few words had helped me at least to buy or ask for something. I've heard people talking about Mozambique. I used to see many people go there for holidays. I couldn't picture this is my mind, Portuguese being one of the main languages spoken in the country.

Few people could speak English and the majority spoke Portuguese. I found lovely people there who had a wide knowledge concerning the value of humanity. There were two American people who approached me, noticing I was a stranger, and spoke English. I had been around for a few days without meeting anyone who could speak English. I was extremely surprised because, at the time, I didn't think there were people who could speak English there due to the majority of the populace speaking Portuguese. Whilst in that surprising time, he addressed me again and immediately we connected. Nevertheless, I had been given something to ponder on – almost unexplainable. We had much to say to each other, after a crucial introduction, with the core of our conversation based on the same point I wrote about which concerns life in exile.

When I met this couple, I was overjoyed and we immediately struck up conversations with great gusto and excitement. The couple took me into their care and carted me off to meet a local Catholic priest at the nearby Catholic Church. Upon meeting the priest, they insisted that he assist me. He accommodated me by taking me to the police station in Maputo. I was taken to a state-owned house where visitors were housed for some time. They housed and fed me. The food was supplied from the Catholic Church. I appreciated this as it had made my journey a little easier.

The American couple checked up on me from time to time after hearing my testimony that everything I had had been stolen. They were moved sympathetically to a point whereby they suggested that I should stay in Mozambique / Maputo, knowing that my idea was to go forward as far as my destination was concerned.

I was heading to London in the United Kingdom but, due to my situation and circumstances, I was unable to pursue my original plan. I had no choice then but to divert to South Africa. I kept this a secret from the couple because they did not want me to go further as they felt I may perish somewhere along the road.

After some time, I still found it difficult to cope in a country where I was unable to communicate effectively in my environment. I told them I had to proceed with my journey to South Africa. Even though they disapproved, they had no choice but to release me. Nevertheless, they provided transportation, wished me well and gave me some directions as to where I could find help, should a problem arise.

Through their help, I was able to reach South Africa. Until then, most of my stories accumulated due to the life I found in South Africa.

Now, here I am in South Africa with a new environment, new life and strange climate. I found myself in the hands of Immigration which is where my journey initiated a life in exile.

A lot of the experience I gained here in South Africa taught me to be a man. A sense of responsibly emerged in me as I found myself being independent and maturing as time went by. This is a consideration I gave myself before gaining it elsewhere. We hardly receive any consideration in times of richness or lack. As we reach times that create consideration in our lives, we then achieve merits that will move us from a certain place to a dimension that opens doors of obtaining consideration from different areas in society.

Many people believe that materialism is the key to consideration and it is well stated by the majority found in modern society. In order to be considered, one needs to have a certain amount of material possessions to deserve respect and awareness. That is how the world begins to consider you.

Prominence in the eyes of the world is not obtained without a price to pay. Journeying on that road needs a lot of camouflaging wherein one will have to divert from the natural to the artificial. The only way that always seems to be more accurate and passive, where consideration is concerned, is when one is considered by the Creator of the universe. That is when one doesn't use much energy.

I felt like a 'nobody' to deserve that type of consideration by Frank and his spouse. I was found in one of the cathedrals before a priest who happened to question me about my destination as well as my origin. It was in a tricky way, trying to find out whether I was a lenient person or what I have come to say as 'streetwise' which means 'con artist', 'manipulator' or, in extreme cases, 'criminal'.

Fortunately, I spoke my heart and he could see, from the bottom of my heart, that what I was telling him was the truth. In another sense, I found this as an opportunity as well and a favour to meet with dignitaries as such.

These three people I had met made my journey smooth to a point whereby I did not dream to proceed abroad because of the consideration I had received. Even once I had reached South Africa, the platform was laid for me to pursue my dream, which was furthering my studies.

I was able to go into tertiary as well as university, obtaining my degrees in both psychology and theology which made my life a lot easier. Through this, the memory of what had transpired became an unforgettable experience, wherein I would also like to convey my thanksgiving to the government of South Africa for making it possible for outsiders to be part of education and certain situations they found themselves part of in the same way as the citizens.

It makes me feel that I am in Africa. As an African, this is how it needs to be whereby we can move everywhere in Africa and find ourselves welcomed as Africans, no matter where we come from or what our colour or ethnic group; but there is always hospitality that is offered to immigrants.

I knew, when I reached here, there were rumours of ill-treatment of immigrants. However, on my side and from my observations, I didn't see it as it had been speculated, but rather that of love and care. The only place where we found a problem was when we were hooked up by the xenophobic attacks which were stimulated politically due to propaganda. This had never happened before except the time when certain local people were intoxicated by attacking their fellow Africans due to hatred attacks and accusations made by the same. On my side, I was a little stupefied by these allegations because, if I had been educated in university, it would have been my time I took and the money for me to be someone in life in order to be correctly positioned.

I didn't understand how somebody who hadn't achieved a certain level of education could allege that I took his position. I believe, if one is a doctor, it's a high qualification which permits him to operate on that same level. However, if a person didn't attain a qualification, he couldn't claim a higher level when he didn't obtain a standard to that level.

Another accusation was that immigrants were taking the local women. This applies to the statement as mentioned above. I believe, if one has discovered the value of humanity and respect the norms thereof, it wouldn't make sense to my observation or analysis of the accusation.

I spent some time looking at things, putting the dots together. In my concept of valuing humanity, women should be considered more as valuable entities due to their position in our lives. They do so much, work hard, are quick to understand and very sympathetic but often they are vulnerable to situations that transpire in society. They are not treated as they should be. That is why my view to this allegation of immigrants taking their women is illogical, as they are not given the consideration they deserve. If there is anyone who gives consideration and value, which should be given to a woman, that gives him the right and full grounds to have that particular woman to love and cherish as she deserves to be.

This is my concern regarding this whole issue. However, other than that, I don't see any other hindrance as far as exile is concerned.

There are different diversities and languages which involve different cultures and traditions, as well as behaviour. Due to this, I cannot claim that many may be wrong in South Africa.

Many times, we forget that the hegemony (superiority) of the humanitarian is in the appointment of God. Regarding human consideration, what I have realised in life is that we should consider one another by putting a very high value on people as we know that, one way or another, we are partners on this earth. In the same consideration, we should learn to take care of others who are unable to vindicate themselves. Thus, this is the true consideration that is needed among us. None of us as human beings are able to occupy even one centimetre of sky, whether rich or poor. We are all children of the soil.

If we consider scientists who have died whilst travelling to other planets, they are always brought back to earth to be buried where others can attend and honour them. Even scientists, as clever as they may be to travel through space, can also die and be brought to the graveyard. Even if they died chronologically (during the period of the earth's existence), it has been the same method given to humanity by the Creator who cares for mankind. We all eventually die. For example, the essential point of this context brings a dynamism of consideration due to the reality that occurs in the world today, due to the selfishness of humanity, whereas it should be one of care for others.

There have been certain routines used by citizens that have affected the majority of people, causing them to neglect others and to be inconsiderate to their fellow human beings and, in the same manner, to abuse their belongings. We should all know that each human deserves consideration. It doesn't matter how one gives it but it has to be given to each and every one.

South Africa has demonstrated a great consideration which makes the majority of people feel that there is a certain amount of care offered to them. There is a certain routine that has taken place by those who want things done so hastily, thus causing it to lose its impact. This is done especially regarding those who have failed to comply with the law.

Chapter 3

Consideration in the marital perspective

Let me stress this point before I touch on my personal experience with regard to marital pacts. Marriage is a significant commitment that involves various considerations to ensure a healthy, fulfilling, and supportive relationship. Here are some key factors to consider in a marital perspective:

Communication

Open Dialogue:
Honest and transparent communication about feelings, expectations, and concerns is critical.

Active Listening:
Truly hearing and understanding each other's viewpoints.

Trust and Honesty

Building Trust:
Trust is the foundation of any strong marriage and must be earnestly cultivated and maintained.

Being Honest:
Honesty fosters trust and integrity in the relationship.

Shared Values and Goals

Common Ground:

Shared values, goals, and beliefs can help in navigating life's challenges together.

Future Planning:
Agreement on key life decisions like finances, children, career aspirations, etc.

Emotional Support

Empathy and Comfort:
Being there for each other emotionally in times of happiness, stress, and sorrow.

Conflict Resolution

Problem Solving:
Effectively managing disagreements through compromise and understanding rather than arguing.

Professional Help:
Willingness to seek counselling or therapy if needed.

Financial Management

Joint Finances:
Understanding and managing shared finances with transparency and mutual agreement.

Financial Goals:
Aligning on financial priorities, such as saving, spending, and investments.

Responsibility and Roles

Shared Duties:
Equitably dividing household responsibilities and other duties.

Flexibility:

Being adaptable to changing roles and responsibilities over time.

Personal Space and Independence

Individual Interests:
Respecting each other's hobbies, interests, and personal time.

Self-growth:
Encouraging individual growth and development.

Intimacy and Affection

Physical Intimacy:
 Maintaining a healthy physical relationship that meets both partners' needs.

Emotional Intimacy:
Building a deep emotional connection and showing affection regularly.

Cultural and Religious Compatibility

Respect:
Respecting each other's cultural and religious backgrounds.

Integration:
Integrating each other's traditions and practices harmoniously.

Extended Family

Boundaries:
Establishing boundaries with in-laws and extended family.

Inclusion:
Including family in your lives but not allowing them to overstep into your marital issues.

Adaptability and Resilience

Life Challenges:
Facing life's ups and downs together with a resilient and adaptable approach.

Flexibility:
Being open to change and willing to grow together through different stages of life.

These considerations can help in building a strong, lasting marital relationship that is based on mutual respect, love, and understanding.

It was a very touching point of my marital scenario that I found in exile. I paid close attention to this side with regarding marital issues. My curiosity rose in certain areas which pushed me to question; but I was unable to answer without help from other speculators.

Thus, this issue had been seen in two ways which brought confusion to my thinking. These ways are seen in true and false contexts. However, its peat because there are some who find vulnerability in the game of those who know deep down that this is the only way to access the priorities found in the country.

In the context of marriage there are so many people who misunderstand, especially those who do it with ulterior motives. They should know that, because of their selfishness, they are ruining other people's lives. However, selfishness involves a price. As far as my conception is concerned, it is fortunate to obtain such a consideration. Thus, it's given in a beneficial way. It is also seen in a deeper manner as far as consideration is concerned.

If I link the point of 'foreign' with the aspect of consideration toward the autochthones of South Africa, there is a certain understanding that is given on this point due to the female side with regard to the wellbeing in a selective manner.

Respect does not play that much of a role with the husband and wife as far as marriage is concerned. There is always confusion on the side of a female. Marital life is not playing to the consideration of both partners, especially on those who are poor. On the other hand, there is a huge gap in the way they concept the marital issue due to the autochthons themselves. There is a good take on it and, on this point, it does not matter to whom it is given.

The other side of my life

My screaming didn't seem to have been considered while I was in the middle of a mass of people. When I called, none heeded. I bit my lips which bled but still received no consideration. I stood with my nagging pain without thinking about colour, language or gender. Then a woman arrived who appeared as an angel. She shook my hand without saying a word and we worked. After sometime, she wanted to know what my screaming was all about. I looked at her with no imaginings or concentration. She then penetrated my mind in a silent vocal tone. Her desire was to know exactly where my sorrow had originated. She wiped away my tears and made me lie down for a while. She said to me, "You can rest a bit." Then, when I awoke, I looked beside the place where I was lying. I saw a sweet smile on her face and she said, "Welcome back." I replied with "Thanks". In my scenarios, I always thought of myself as being smart.

Looking deeper into my life in exile while living in South Africa, angels of delusion surrounded me on all fronts. I was humbled while living in exile and found myself distracted and thrown off balance in my thinking as unpleasant thoughts buffeted my judgments in a strange way, getting me to think that it was good and attractive to follow this type of thinking and living. I could feel myself being pushed in a direction but did not know my destination. This was a mystery to me. My self-esteem dropped and I knew I had lost the ability to speak – which came as a huge surprise to me!

When it appeared that people were ignoring my dilemma,

my strength left me. The kind lady, who had had compassion on me, led me to a refreshing stream, bringing me back to the place of restoration.

That scenario of my life caused me to doubt everything that had come my way after being deceived and being used like a remote control. I felt regret for having trusted humans. This was unexplainable to those who had seen me marvel at my situation.

It took me two years living in the lies of my girlfriend after she had given birth to the baby, telling me that it was mine. I had done my best to ensure the innocent baby remained healthy. For me, being in exile was very tough, being a student without any resource that would allow me to have money. My focus was on the growth of this baby. It was a two-year struggle for me.

One morning, I received a phone call. A male voice asked me who I was. I spoke to the gentleman, giving him my name. He told me it was expensive to talk over the phone and wanted to see me. When I first met the man, he was very angry. However, after our conversation, he understood I had shown no indication of being the father of the baby. He then told me he was one of the three men who could be the father of this baby. In this entire scenario, her game was based on money. After all, we, the three 'could be fathers', had to pay different amounts as maintenance.

I received the grace to become acquainted with this other man in a proper way because I knew him as the father of this 'angel' (girlfriend). It amazed me that I was the one whom he kept calling. The phone was programmed 'father' as the man's name. The other man worked near my home. His name was programmed 'uncle'. They used to meet at month ends. I could see that, whenever she came back from the first man, her requested amount was approximately R1 500 monthly. The second man was being charged approximately R1 000 monthly. The amount I was being charged was

R700. All in all, she scored about R3 200. Her earnings were surpassing many who worked at various companies.

After having been through all this, I began to grow into maturity. Knowing a bit concerning life, this brought me to a concept that raised my self-esteem to a sense of being serious about life although I've written this book, feeling the same as I was, having still been found in exile. After understanding myself more, that is what my emotions reflected, having been away from my own country with pain and sorrow as well as nostalgia.

When I used to be under my parents' roof, it was impossible to come up with such experience. However, being away from my own home gave me a lot of 'know-how'.

The following chapter also shows the emotions that come from the pressure of life in exile, which will stimulate readers, learning from someone who had heard of exile without understanding the gravity thereof. I believe this book will offer you a better comprehension regarding the lives of those who are found in exile. You may have seen them around you without knowing how they live their lives.

In the conceptualisation of this book, there is dynamism in the ideas that attribute to the feedback of the reality seen in the reading thereof as well as the understanding found in the chapters. It can also be linked with certain thought patterns which reflect the nature of life and its irony. This is not about saying, "I've seen it" or "I've heard of it". Rather, it's about saying how we've been through it by living in it for so long and having felt the pressure thereof in all walks of life.

Chapter 4

The pressure of life in exile

Life in exile brings a unique set of pressures and challenges that can weigh heavily on an individual. Being forced to leave one's home country – whether due to political persecution, conflict, or other forms of adversity – often results in profound emotional, psychological, and social strains.

Emotional and Psychological Strain

Loss of Identity and Belonging:
Leaving behind familiar surroundings, cultural norms, and communities can result in a sense of dislocation and loss of identity. Exiles often struggle to find their place in a new society, which can lead to feelings of isolation and loneliness.

Trauma and Anxiety:
The circumstances that lead to exile are often traumatic. Witnessing violence, experiencing persecution, or losing loved ones can leave deep emotional scars. The uncertainty of the future in exile can also lead to chronic anxiety.

Homesickness and Grief:
Missing home, family, and friends is a constant ache for many in exile. There is often a deep, enduring sense of grief and longing for the life left behind.

Social and Economic Challenges

Cultural Adaptation:
Adjusting to a new culture can be challenging. Language barriers, different social norms, and unfamiliar legal systems can create significant obstacles to integration.

Legal Status and Rights:
Depending on the country of asylum, exiles may face uncertain or precarious legal status. This uncertainty can affect their ability to work, access healthcare, and participate fully in society.

Economic Hardship:
Exiles often face economic challenges, such as finding employment, securing housing, and meeting basic needs. Professional qualifications and experiences may not be recognised, forcing individuals to take low-paying or unskilled jobs.

Resilience and Adaptation

Despite these overwhelming challenges, many people in exile demonstrate remarkable resilience. Building new communities, pursuing education, and seeking opportunities for personal growth are ways individuals cope and adapt to their new circumstances.

Community Support:
Exiles often find support and solidarity within diaspora communities that share similar experiences, providing a network for mutual aid, cultural continuity, and emotional support.

Advocacy and Activism:
Some exiles use their experiences to become advocates for human rights, drawing attention to the issues that forced them into exile and working towards systemic change.

The pressure of life in exile is multifaceted and deeply personal, affecting every aspect of an individual's existence. Navigating these pressures requires strength, resilience, and often the support of compassionate communities and organizations. Recognising the struggles faced by those in exile can foster a more inclusive and supportive environment, helping them rebuild their lives with dignity and hope.

My opinion concerning the pressures of life is not referring to pressure we undergo when we have certain work to do. It's more psychological pressure that one undergoes due to life in exile. It has been almost 20 years since I left my native country. Herein, I have faced a lot and persisted more than my age could allow me; more than one would usually experience.

These 20 years have been hectic in training, education and torture. I understand what pain, hunger and suffering is.

I grasped what it is to struggle. I learnt much through this sphere of life in over two decades in exile. South Africa has become my home due to the challenge and adversities that I have come across. I have decided to settle though my zeal was to go further. However, due to my age, I knew that time is going fast and there's not enough space to redeem it.

Since I found myself forming my nuclear family around me, I made it my decision to settle and no longer be the vagabond in my mind, spirit and body. I believe stability is the key to success.

I have been in more than eight countries around Africa. I faced different challenges in all these places with their different cultures and customs, one being Rwanda. I visited there in 1999. It was a good place for tourism. My visit wasn't that long but, in the short time I was there, I was able to experience new things which built my awareness concerning life outside my native country.

The first thing I experienced was finding myself in a particular place without parents. This made me feel that I was man enough at the age of twenty-four. It frightened me but I had no choice and this is how I have been on my own in a foreign country. Whilst I had no friends or relatives to lean on, the only thing I had with me was the itinerary to my destination which helped me focus on the places I had in mind as far as going forward was concerned.

I believed that going to Europe, Asia or outside Africa meant peace to me but I learned later that it's the same everywhere – except in Heaven. The whole world contains the same challenges, especially when one is found in a new place with new people and a new culture. There is a huge challenge as one begins to adapt. It's more like starting life from the beginning. However, I viewed this as a waste of time. As much as I needed to adjust in life, I understood that adjustments are within the mind – not the place. Man was created to be content in whatever situation he would find himself.

I understood that life is the same all over the world. However, what motivated me most to attain stability in South Africa was the responsibility to become a leader of a certain demographic group. That calmed me and made me more careful about my decision not to tour the world any further.

This was my inspiration facing the world which would connect me to the necessary channels and allow me to express my feelings to writers through my experience in life, while in exile.

During this time, I have gained experience and can enlighten those who have not been in exile. Therefore, this had to do with things I have undergone due to pain and troubles wherein I was strengthened. I can now resolve things through experience and wisdom as well as age.

The trouble we face expands our intellectual capacity and we must spend time wisely as every moment is beneficial. It speeded up my thinking process. One's mind can progress in advance. I could not afford to be left behind in thought, opportunity or in any other way.

If people have been spoiled in the past and, thereafter, life becomes tough, they don't want to move forward. Such a person desires to continue living in the past, not wanting to experience anything new and thus begins to regress. This cripples one's life and progress. One becomes limited mentally, spiritually and physically. A person's life cannot depend on souvenirs. We must not look to the past.

Look to the future. Thinking ahead makes us futuristic. That's how we overcome mental limitations and obstacles that impose themselves on us at any given time. The future has a package of its own enhancement whereas the past brings stagnation.

In life, we learn to move forward with the speed of success, not the slowness of failure because, once we are dominated by failure, it places limitations on our lives. This slows us down and hinders progress, which then leads to giving up and can result in being suicidal. The remedy to this is to live one's life daily being hopeful, knowing that one is not born to fail. This will take us to our destiny and prevent us from being hindered by our emotions and illusions.

Another place where I experienced some challenges was Bujumbura Burundi. It was not easy during the time of my visit there.

Life wasn't easy. There was always pressure. Corruption was their 'password' at that time. I recall one day when I was robbed whilst walking in town. This was one of the worst experiences I had ever been through. The thief stole what was precious to me. I felt disorientated from being at Immigration. This thief was tall. I didn't know who to call on as I was a stranger in a foreign country. All I could do was endure the pain and view this experience as a learning curve.

I found it difficult to move forward. My destination was well determined but I battled to go on. This was a huge scenario I hadn't experienced before. I was found in the middle of nowhere, with not a penny on me.

According to my destination, Burundi was still too far off. I looked to my right and left but I couldn't see any other way except to seek help from above. At that point, life seemed hopeless. My strength appeared to weaken and my vision became dim. I became doubtful about my plans. I had questions, some of which hindered my progress. I have learned lessons during the pressures of life and I attempted to apply some of them to the best of my ability, wherein I gained experience.

Thus, the only way to overcome the pressures of life is to go through them. Life under the pressure of exile tends to have another hard side of its own, especially when we link this to what we see and feel by the resulting reality that occurs around us. It gives the meaning of what pressure is, using a metaphoric process in the manner of analysing what is found easily and what is found with difficulty. However, the harshness of exile is realistically where the access of life is appreciated.

In the same stead, I believe the pressures of life determine whether we decide to continue or give up. My understanding is based on the way I struggled to the point where I was found outside my country. This happened when I went to prison due to my being a car guard in an area that wasn't acceptable. We had battled to find a place where we could guard cars so we worked wherever we could find them. I didn't know there were laws and limitations pertaining to this. At this point, the police arrived, requesting money and I told them that was like trying to get milk from a bull. Thereafter, we were dragged onto a truck and transported to prison for a few days where after we were released. This made me think much because it was one problem after the other. I had double trouble following me every step I took.

Somehow, I took this as a curse following me as it seemed everything was blocked. I had been pressurised in more than nine countries in Africa. Each had different types of pressures and all these accumulated to my solidity in experience and my way of viewing things. Frequently, some people forget there can never be any type of happiness without embracing life's pressures. In my own experience, I have learnt this, having gone through high pressure situations.

At times, circumstances took me completely by surprise and I found myself losing control of my plans. However, when I came to the knowledge of how life is at times, I used those opportunities to discipline myself which taught me to endure any type of pressure. Everything seemed blocked but, later on, I understood there is no formula for life, neither for the rich nor the poor. We may have plenty today and tomorrow we may have nothing. That's how life can be.

I found it very difficult on my own, especially when I began to understand emergency situations such as becoming ill. Unfortunately, if one encounters medical expenses and has insufficient funds or lack of family, one will find it difficult to cope. This is one of the pressures we have to embrace at times when we don't have parents or any relatives who can assist.

Pressure leads us to deviate from our goals and visions. These pressures can move us from the ideals we have envisioned. This can lead us to take shortcuts, many of which can lead to problems that can corner us for a long time. It's not easy to accurately recall what we have been through which is why there are many incomplete stories. Regardless of how we view our past, we will not be able to analyse everything. However, when I undergo this type of pressure, I then find myself doing what I hadn't previously thought of.

That is where many exiled, finding themselves practising evil. It wasn't easy being found in the situation whereby I began to view my future negatively. Between the ages of 32 and 35, my life was in a shambles. I didn't know how to pick up the pieces because I was all over the show. The only time

I was able to gather myself was when I experienced that life has no formula and that's when I stood up and refused to speak negative words over my life.

I began to speak *life* over myself. I told myself I would make it and that's when I found myself moving forward and leaving failure and confusion behind me. I began to engage in positive steps. In addition to this, I became successful – not because I studied at a high level, but because I increased in understanding.

I understood the rhythm of life and this projected me further. I studied and qualified as a psychologist but that was inadequate. I went further and achieved a high qualification in philosophy – a master's degree – but that was also inadequate. Later on, I walked in my determination of facing life wasn't enough because I was still living in the past.

I refused to embrace the future and, due to that, I was crippled mentally until I realised my potential. That's when I said enough was enough. I can now stand and speak life as well as sense to the world, both spiritually and intellectually. My ability also allowed me to speak in world politics and religious points of view. All this occurred during my life in South Africa, life without any occupation, when there were bills to be paid every month.

When we experience pressure, there is always a sense of hopelessness and, when hope is gone, we tend to lose confidence. Fear takes hold and life becomes frustrating. Lack of control influences our decisions. All we see is darkness and have a negative view of the future, assuming it won't stop. Why do we struggle with pressure? Is it that we do not have tactics to conquer it or do we think we're not good enough to overcome it? This should be a question to ask yourself as you read this book. I believe the only way to experience relief from this type of pressure is to admit that we need help.

Most people do not understand this when they are facing

pressure. This has been a routine in some people's lives. They keep going through this cycle over and over and this causes defeat in their lives. There are certain things that one should not allow to become a habit in one's life.

Such problems should not be stored in one's heart because they are like acid. The more we store them, the deeper they excavate into our hearts. That's where many people's health declines due to problems they have been holding onto for so long. Then, when the heart cannot handle it any longer, it becomes a problem. My advice to you is to let go of whatever burdens your heart in order to create a space for new things therein.

Remember, your heart is not a wagon to pile everything on until you can't handle the weight of it. Handle one problem at a time. The solution is thus as follows. We must speak out what our hearts are laden with. Speak to a close friend or professional. This is what it means to let go. Our environment adapts to the life we manage. One cannot hide what is building up in the heart. Whatever the heart is filled with will come out of the mouth. When the inner man is fed up, that's when the outer man tends to manifest the emotions.

When something is building up in me, my reactions will be aggressive and expressive and one can see that my heart is too burdened. Whatever happens in our lives, we too often tend to blame an event. We don't normally blame ourselves and examine our own behaviour. How did it happen? With any situation that occurs in life, one has to engage in a monologue and that will require introspection. In the African context, there are always those to blame and many people tend to blame their forefathers as well as their ancestors.

Few appear to come up with reasons concerning the season. After a while, I became confused, having found myself in the same trap. The anticipation of most people relies on optimism that is pushed by the longevity of a situation surrounding them at that particular time. There are times when the pressure of life lingers to an extent where I try to find a quicker solution by expressing those feelings to a close friend. Sometimes we ask for advice from people but they haven't waited for us to come to them so they can break us down.

Pressure in the academic world

In the academic world, there were too many challenges I was unable to face on my own. These needed an external helping hand as far as life was concerned. I couldn't imagine the whole struggle during my studies at the University of South Africa. I tried to cope with academic pressure as well as financial struggles. Thankfully, these situations worked in my favour as I persevered. This made me much stronger. Who really knows what things one could go through?

Initially, my life seemed promising but later things changed. My situation made me feel incompetent, whereas I had the capacity to prove myself academically. Yet, because of the circumstances I found myself in, I couldn't meet the requirements as far as my studies were concerned. However, as time passed, I managed to break through as I obtained my master's degree in philosophy. This gave me hope and I became more ambitious. It became a lesson that I most desired, to teach or inform those going through the same situation to never lose hope.

One must always have the hope of making it in the future as I did. It took time to prove myself due to the system, terms and conditions that are found in exile. To co-operate with the system, I had to move at their speed rate. However, I encountered challenges that I wasn't supposed to face but it taught me to understand the only thing you cannot fight in life is the system. This matured me and eventually I made it. This was not by my power but by the power of the Most High God. My first semester was very tough because I had financial difficulties which hindered me from focusing on my academic work.

I hadn't obtained help from anybody. This took place over

three months until my brother, Paul Black, took charge of my expenses. We cannot be oblivious when it's time to share what we've been through. If we don't, this can return any time in the future as it's known that, when we don't speak about what has hooked us, the return thereof will increase the pressure which can attack so many areas of life.

What response do people have toward pressure? This question doesn't seem to get the proper response. So many respond differently. However, it does point to the stronghold which afflicts one psychologically. This is one of the serious cases that arises in our lives wherein most people are unable to find answers. Sometimes, we project ignorance, forgetting those little things we disregard which can cause pressure and destroy a person. We focus more on bigger problems than these smaller ones. This is something that can cause life to be uncomfortable and we must get rid of it.

I recall days when I struggled to earn money that could enable me to pay my bills. I was employed by *Pro Force* in South Africa to install alarms while under pressure to continue with my studies. I was also put under pressure by a manager of *Pro Force*. When my exams were due, I informed this man who was then very quick to deduct from my salary each month. He told me not to make my problem theirs. This taught me a lot. I learnt that my problems were mine.

Sometimes we want people to be sympathetic to us when it means nothing to them. When we explain things, hoping they will assist us, their response is almost always negative. There are people who won't listen to our stories. Instead, they break us down and embarrass us. As a student, I could work from Monday to Friday. It was difficult to focus on my studies, all of which was because I didn't have an alternative. I depended on myself to survive. When my salary was paid late, I decided to resign from the company.

I joined another organisation and that's where I began to

stand up for myself. I was trained in electronics and to repair all types of appliances. This was a long run for me due to my studies and I was eventually able to sponsor myself with the level of credentials I had obtained. The difficulties that came were at a speed I couldn't handle. Then I cried out in anguish, asking life what I had done to deserve it but there was no answer.

I desperately sought help but none seemed to arrive. Later on, I learned that pressure does not regard size or respect anybody. It comes to all humans. Whether big or small, rich or poor, all are found with the same challenges.

Chapter 5

Accessibility in exile and motive

Exile is a complex experience shaped by manifold factors, including the motives behind it and the accessibility to resources and support in the host country. Understanding these dimensions is crucial for comprehending the challenges faced by individuals in exile and for developing effective support mechanisms.

Motives for Exile

Political Persecution:
Many individuals are forced into exile due to political reasons. They may be activists, journalists, or dissidents who face threats, imprisonment, or even death in their home countries. Their motives are often rooted in the desire for freedom, human rights, and justice.

Conflict and Violence:
War, ethnic conflicts, and violence can drive people from their homes. These individuals seek safety and protection from the immediate danger of armed conflict or targeted violence.

Economic Hardship:
Severe economic conditions, lack of opportunities, and extreme poverty can lead to exile. This is often seen in cases where individuals seek better living conditions

and opportunities for themselves and their families.

Environmental Factors:
Environmental disasters, such as droughts, floods, and hurricanes, can force communities to leave their homes. Climate change is increasingly becoming a significant factor behind forced migrations.

Discrimination and Identity-Based Persecution:
Persecution based on race, religion, ethnicity, gender, or sexual orientation can also compel individuals to leave their home countries in search of safer, more accepting environments.

Accessibility in the Host Country

Legal Status:
The legal status accorded to exiles – whether as refugees, asylum seekers, or undocumented immigrants – plays a crucial role in determining their access to resources. Legal recognition can provide pathways to work authorization, residency, and citizenship, whereas a lack of legal status can lead to vulnerability and exploitation.

Social Services:
Access to social services such as healthcare, education, and housing support is critical. Host countries vary widely in the provisions they make for exiles, with some offering comprehensive support and others providing minimal assistance.

Employment:
Finding stable employment can be challenging. Legal barriers, language proficiency, and non-recognition of foreign qualifications often limit job opportunities. Support in job placement and skills training can help mitigate these issues.

Language and Cultural Integration:

Language proficiency is a major barrier to integration. Host countries that offer language classes, cultural orientation programs, and community support networks can facilitate smoother transitions and better integration for exiles.

Community and Social Networks:
The presence of diaspora communities and other supportive networks can significantly impact the experience of exile. These networks offer emotional support, cultural continuity, and practical assistance in navigating life in the new country.

Mental Health Support:
The traumas that lead to and are experienced during exile necessitate robust mental health support. Access to counselling and mental health services can be crucial for dealing with past traumas and current stressors.

Balancing Motives and Accessibility

Policy Implications:
Governments and organizations need to understand the diverse motives behind exile to tailor appropriate support services. Policies should aim to provide comprehensive support encompassing legal recognition, social services, employment assistance, and mental health care.

Advocacy and Awareness:
Raising awareness about the plight of exiles can lead to more compassionate and informed communities. Advocacy efforts can push for more inclusive policies and better support systems.

Community Initiatives:
Grassroots organizations and community groups often play vital roles in bridging gaps left by formal systems. These initiatives can offer immediate, context-specific support and empower exiles.

The motives behind exile and accessibility in the host country are deeply intertwined factors that shape the exile experience. A nuanced understanding of these aspects can inform better policies and support mechanisms, helping individuals in exile rebuild their lives with dignity and hope. By addressing both the reasons that drive people into exile and the barriers they face in new environments, we can work towards creating more inclusive and supportive societies.

The word 'access' can be used in different contexts, depending on the user, when or where to employ the word. In other terms, it is a condition of 'being accessible'. However, if I ponder on the same word, I find myself coming up with different conceptions as far as my context is concerned. The word 'access' in this chapter is personalised within the concept of the situation that is found in exile.

With this, I will have various approaches which clarify the comprehension of the chapter within it.

There is a fundamental approach, however, when the 'access' manifests to an individual, causing supernatural feelings which bring philosophical thoughts, favouring success which takes place in reality.

My first access that I found in life while in exile was through the documents I was first offered in South Africa. These made me accountable to the people living in the country at that time.

I was amongst millions of immigrants and nonimmigrants. Most people take life differently, particularly those who are unable to identify who or what they are. I found this so difficult to understand as I was still lonely and, simultaneously, feeling rejection even though I wasn't rejected. All that occupied me were worries and questions that seemed unstoppable. All the opportunities I grasped were very significant and also disappointing.

I used to be so excited after being called for an interview concerning employment because my accesses were limited. Life became so hard with a tangible element in my mind's eye.

My strength began to diminish when my desired plans seemed to be thwarted. My hope turned to sadness, my eyes were greatly opened and I shifted to a position wherein there was no time for curiosity.

After all the atrocities of life and their irony, I learnt to take whatever came my way. This lifted me to a certain dimension whereby I had to know myself better than I thought I did. Time moved on to a point where lies seemed to be the truth, when today became tomorrow, the future became the past and yesterday became history. At that time, I found the impossible becoming possible. It was then that benevolence approached me with remarkable insight.

I gave time for my imagination to work in order to envision an impacting idea. Suddenly, the light of hope and my strength returned and my visuals clearly opened. The access I obtained came from an unexpected source and I was encouraged.

When considering the little success I had obtained outside my native country, my opportunities were limited as I was an immigrant. This caused me to have a tough time because I had not yet furthered my studies. My priorities hinged on the legality I had due to the documents I possessed. For eight years I had been living in Africa, learning and comparing the accessibilities which surrounded me while living there. I changed my status to refugee as I kept my real identity hidden, being Jamaican. Due to the obstacles I experienced when I was in central Africa DRC, I thought I would end up in jail for not meeting the conditions of living in Africa.

I wasn't prepared for any uncertain events as I believed my safety was well secured. My zeal only rose because I had found my success. However, I came across a large mountain that wouldn't allow me to progress which took most of my time when I could have been doing something solid. I left Jamaica though I was only nineteen, due to showing up to fulfil the promise that we had of living successfully. This was based on our education in order to stay focused by grooming us into our future. This affirmed that whoever passed their classes during primary school would be granted a chance to go to Africa to further their secondary schooling. Then my dreams became reality. Opportunities arose as I found myself where I wanted to be in life, even though what we mostly desired didn't occur exactly as we thought.

When I had an opportunity to go to the Congo, it was a great privilege for me although obstacles arose at the time which I was to take more seriously. The triviality of the moment couldn't permit me to use all my opportunities while my access began to open. That's when I met with tough times. In my seventh year living in DRC, the war began and I couldn't risk my life staying in the country. This was a severe war which began in 1996. I decided to leave. At that time, things worsened. We ran as there were no cars allowed to be driven around and this made it even more difficult. I reached a stage where I had to walk 190 kilometers with a little six-year-old child in my arms. I found myself unable to carry the little boy. I had to make him walk as well.

Thus, it was a confusing time which I hadn't experienced before. I tried to make a plan to avoid becoming too tired. I had much luggage to carry. I tried to find help but it wasn't easy because every person had their own situation. At that time, if I had asked anyone for help, I could have been killed by those same people because everybody was suffering. Some had lost their kids, others had lost wealth and friends.

There were more than two million people on the same route. We had to spend two days walking approximately seven kilometers on the narrow road where multimillionaires were walking with us.

I could never have known or reached them in any other way

but, at that time, they were on my side. After a while, we found ourselves in a place called Kabare – a little township which people had vacated a week prior. The people there had become aware of the danger that had developed. We arrived there at approximately 20H15, having left our homes at about 10H00 the day before.

We found a resting place. We couldn't find anywhere to buy food. A hungry little boy began to cry. I tried to ignore him but he cried out repeatedly. None of us had eaten for two days. During the time we walked, we had to ignore our hunger as we pushed on in order to save our lives. Fortunately, there were people who heard this boy crying for food. They gave him some biscuits which calmed him. The boy's mother couldn't be found since we had left. It was only six months later that we discovered she was still alive, when we were able to contact people regarding those who had been lost after the war began to diminish.

We tried to find a way to escape from the place, having been on the run for three weeks. We were told the only place to access travel was from Bunya. This was approximately 250 kilometers away. At that time, I had no documentation that would allow me to travel. I had thrown all my belongings away. All I had were the clothes I had put on four months prior. By the time I had walked about a 120 kilometers, my feet started to swell. The six-year-old boy was still strong which surprised me. We walked day and night. I carried my bag on my back with other luggage on my head whilst holding a little baby to prevent him from getting lost.

All I had in my mind was that I would walk until I dropped dead somewhere because I had already lost hope of living. A little boy helped me to understand many things at that time. I considered him as my guardian angel. This boy had recovered from malnutrition. I battled to believe he could walk that distance. The child was keeping me from doing something bad to myself, as I already had in mind to just terminate my life to avoid the next bout of trouble that would come my way. This boy spoke to me by showing that, when he reached the destination, he would tell the story to his friends about what we had been through.

The amazing feat was more up hills than straights. It involved climbing mountains for about two hours. That was when I wanted to throw away what I had. I was among a few people who were still carrying their belongings. I tried to throw away some of my things which I had been carrying until I found myself empty-handed.

I'd even thrown away my passport and ID when I had walked for about two weeks without having something in my hands except the little boy. Sometimes we can long to be somewhere but that place may become a disaster zone. We can end up being miserable due to our self-satisfaction if we don't pay attention.

My situation was in the radical struggle which had made me lose consideration of all the things I had which had brought certainty to my future to be bright as far as qualifications were concerned. I ended up losing all my documents due to war pressure. The only thing I didn't lose was my matric certificate because it was in a bag the boy carried. This became one of the biggest obstacles that I've ever experienced. I failed to accomplish most of my plans because I had been unable to gain access to most of the things I had hoped for in life. Therefore, I didn't strive to find the reason why my ambitions would not flourish.

I believe there are those who have been through all these things, reaching the same sense of hopelessness. They lose sight of hope. There seems to be nothing else but to terminate their lives. My attribution of the crises you may have been going through is to offer you a type of braveness found in my book which contains what I've experienced in life.

You may have some situations and, without knowing what

they all are, all you can do is discover what sort of obstacles you're facing. They may not be similar to mine but, as long as it reflects on something that hinders progress in your life, get real and trace it before it's too late. Try to come up with a solution because it is within you.

We do come across terrific crises that surpass our capacity of comprehension. We then struggle to come up with solutions. However, the only way we can help ourselves is when we accept that we're facing challenges which are categorised in a certain dimension that occupies a large space within us. In addition to this, if we learn to confidentially deal with them without losing control, that's when we then conquer those challenges we are facing.

It's unusual to find people controlling their situation, who are willing to deal with it personally, until they are over it, having found relief through the effort they made. Somehow, our responses may look different when we discover something is not right within us. We try to link it without success as I did when I was in a sense of hopelessness. However, through that little boy I had run with in an attempt to escape the war, I managed to succeed instead of giving in to failure.

Chapter 6

Mutual love toward immigrants and refugees in exile

This chapter is about what we normally go through and how we consider one another in terms of showing love and respect.

Mutual love toward immigrants and refugees in exile can profoundly enhance their quality of life, foster integration, and enrich the host communities. This mutual love and support can manifest in various forms, ranging from empathetic policies to grassroots community initiatives. Here's an exploration of how this can be nurtured and what benefits it brings to both immigrants, refugees, and the host society.

Government and Policy-Level Support

Inclusive Policies:
Governments can design policies that are inclusive and supportive of immigrants and refugees. This includes providing legal pathways for residency and citizenship, access to social services, and protection against discrimination.

Humanitarian Aid and Resettlement Programs:
Governments and international organizations can work together to develop robust resettlement programs, ensuring

that refugees and immigrants have safe living conditions, access to healthcare, education, and employment opportunities.

Community Engagement:
Politicians and local leaders can actively engage with immigrant communities, seeking their input on policies that affect them and fostering a culture of inclusion and mutual respect.

Community and Grassroots Initiatives

Welcome Programs:
Community-run welcome programs can help immigrants and refugees settle in, offering services such as language classes, cultural orientation, and practical assistance with housing and employment.

Cultural Exchange Events:
Creating opportunities for cultural exchange, such as festivals, food fairs, and art exhibitions, can help build mutual understanding and respect between immigrants and the host community.

Mentorship and Support Networks:
Local residents can volunteer to become mentors for newcomers, offering guidance, friendship, and support as they navigate their new environment.

Education and Awareness

Educational Programs:
Schools and universities can play a pivotal role by including curricula that promote understanding and appreciation of different cultures and the challenges faced by immigrants and refugees.

Public Awareness Campaigns:
Media and community organizations can run campaigns

that highlight the contributions of immigrants and refugees, debunk myths, and promote a narrative of inclusion and mutual respect.

Personal and Interpersonal Connections

Building Relationships:
Individual acts of kindness and friendship can make a significant difference. Taking the time to listen to and understand the experiences of immigrants and refugees fosters empathy and mutual respect.

Volunteerism:
Volunteering with organizations that support immigrants and refugees, such as language programs or job training centers, can provide invaluable assistance and create strong community bonds.

Benefits of Mutual Love and Support

Enhanced Well-Being:
Immigrants and refugees who feel welcomed and supported are more likely to experience improved mental and emotional well-being. This sense of belonging can mitigate the trauma and stress associated with displacement.

Successful Integration:
Love and support from the host community can greatly facilitate the integration process. When immigrants and refugees feel included, they are more likely to contribute positively to society, enriching it with their skills, perspectives, and cultures.

Social Cohesion:
Mutual respect and understanding foster a sense of unity and cohesion within communities. This can lead to more harmonious social interactions and a strong, diverse community fabric.

Economic and Cultural Benefits:
Immigrants and refugees can bring significant economic benefits, filling labor gaps, and contributing to innovation and entrepreneurship. Culturally, they add to the richness of society, offering new perspectives and traditions.

Mutual love toward immigrants and refugees in exile involves empathy, understanding, and proactive support at multiple levels – government, community, and individual. By nurturing these bonds, we build stronger, more inclusive communities where everyone has the opportunity to thrive. This mutual support not only benefits immigrants and refugees but also enriches the host society, creating a more diverse, dynamic, and resilient community.

Now, South Africa has many who are in exile. Thus, it was difficult to come up with an accurate guess regarding nations found there. However, I couldn't count them because there are so many people from all over the world, not all of them being immigrants.

Most people are involved in business, some are studying and the rest are refugees. Everyone has different motives, each of them experiencing difficulties of their own. Each individual has his own grievances. There are reasons why people burnish their native places. Are we all abiding in love for one another and, if not, why aren't we? Many times, I failed to give an appropriate answer to this type of question. Thus, it was posed at the right time as well as relevant to this chapter. The goal hereof is to better understand the position of those in exile. Thus, in order to do this well, we need to give ourselves some time to become acquainted with the feelings of being in exile. Life in exile concerns many things we sometimes cannot relate to.

I have closely considered what I've suffered, namely the indignity of keeping my dignity, something others may have practised daily. This is because I believe in self-respect. I can only respect others if it begins within myself. Most of my experiences were in South Africa and DRC, the other place where I've spent a lot of time.

Is love applicable toward those who are in exile? This was one of my daily questions, after seeing what goes on in each and every individual. People pay much attention to their own lives rather than giving it even to those around them. Most people living in exile believe the only time to give attention to others is when it is given to them.

I was convinced the only way to show love to someone was when I gave attention to that particular person. If we don't love something, we are unlikely to give attention to it. As I've seen in various ways, it's within ourselves and our attitudes to demonstrate and share love with others. Our facial expressions indicate if we are showing love or not. To demonstrate love in exile requires a huge effort, as there are so many people in exile worldwide. This is where one needs to start sharing true love, from the beginning.

If I can't help somebody then I cannot do much to help them at all. With this in mind, there are those who could not stand the kind of life we lived which resulted in failure. I recall myself doing some research, interviewing some of the refugees who were studying at universities and those who were still writing matric.

This situation was about getting to know how they felt in obtaining their own independence. I was given different views from many individuals whom I interviewed. The results I received were from two different categories – one being complaints about being abused by the government for not responding to their needs in accordance with the agreement the government had given to refugees living in South Africa.

Though there were various grievances, it sounded like one voice which showed the pain and sorrow within them. After reaching the root of their complaints, it became quite complex. I then sympathised with them, as one who was dragged into a bad situation. It seemed unfair.

After having been informed that there was an agreement between the government and UNCHR, I had to agree with these views. It was decided that refugees were allowed to study and have a place to live. However, in all this, I've haven't seen any so-called help take place with my own eyes. This was abominable. All in all, I didn't want to come up with uncertainties. It was better for me to do more research concerning the services of the country.

Regarding the routines of Home Affairs, I discovered this place was like another world compared to what it used to be. It brought back nostalgic memories to people about the good times and peace which existed in those days. Most refugees had their contracts terminated as they battled to get documents which would allow them to continue working.

Some managers failed to understand the situation as they wanted to benefit themselves from the services provided. That's when I understood where the hatred was derived from within those who are in exile in South Africa and elsewhere. Often, situations tend to change people from natural to artificial behaviour which invites all sorts of atrocities they weren't born with. I believe there is no one who came from his or her mother's womb being qualified as a criminal or with other horrible behaviour. All these were caused by having no support within the South African Government. We were all innocently born into this world, created by God. Adam was the first man created who was tempted by the devil and fell into sin.

This is one of the main reasons which pushes me to state that, whatever took place within refugees, was caused by misery they were living in. Their first love was constrained, which affected them psychologically, due to the pressure in their lives. The persecution that most refugees had undergone was due to being unable to gain access to so many things.

Life was fair for those in exile but the systems in place were not favourable for refugees concerning their right of living. There were many who had lost their spirit of confraternity and companionship as life had become very difficult for them. In addition to this, it caused great pain rather than bringing peace and stability. As stated in the previous chapter, love was lost for the people who were found in exile.

Socrates, an ancient Greek philosopher, had questions to ask people in order to measure their capability of understanding by asking, *"What is love?"* Most of us are able to respond to this question because it was well practised within our families. (The real answer is – *'God is Love'*).

Mutual love was no longer applied to the lives of those found in exile. Their concept of love had gone, having been substituted by hatred and jealousy-fueled competition. Therefore, they couldn't do the right thing for one another and, if they had to, it had to be paid back in return. I was so inspired by this philosopher; thus, his questions took my thoughts to another realisation of life.

Socrates asked a second question which was very relevant to our daily life, namely "What is truth?" Many times, we fail to apply the truth because of the situation we're facing, losing our sense of humour, thinking the truth won't satisfy our desires. When people become enemies of truth, they won't care about what we think. Yet, they remain that way due to the fear within them, being that they will lose what they have if they face their fear. What can truth lead us to? Humanity has need of putting on truth as one of the greatest materials, bringing a healthy self-esteem. When our demeanour is positive, it reflects our character which makes us likeable to others.

The truth is about honesty and, in addition, we can develop a sense of trustworthiness within a spirit of verity that we keep alight in our lives. If we can think 'truth' in the sense of how God created the universe, we shall identify with it as opposed to what scientists state regarding myths explaining things. Some stories are myths regarding how the creation and human beings came into existence. However, it is seen that even the earth contains truth. So why not us? I tried to live in truth even though conditions hindered it. I had to battle with failure, unaware that victory would come through some of these challenges.

The key to justice is truth. I remember attending a court case in order to testify on behalf of one of my roommates whose home language was French. As a refugee, he had been jailed in South Africa. In order to help him, the first thing I did was enquire as to why he had been detained. He explained in detail why he went to jail. Based on the main reason, the only way I could assist was to advise him to put on the garment of truth as most of his defence was based on lies. One of his excuses was: "My friend, you know the conditions we live in. If I tell the truth, I'll end up being in jail for years." My reply to him was: "Just stick with verity. Don't you worry." He was finally released just because of the truth that he had spoken.

Chapter 7

How to endure in exile

Enduring exile can be an incredibly challenging and emotionally taxing experience. Whether driven by political, social, economic, or environmental factors, living away from one's home country often involves significant adjustment and hardship. However, there are strategies and resources that can help individuals navigate and endure these challenges. Here are some comprehensive approaches:

Emotional and Psychological Resilience

Acknowledge Your Emotions:
It's important to recognize and accept feelings of loss, grief, frustration, and anxiety. Suppressing these emotions can lead to further mental health issues.

Seek Professional Help:
Accessing mental health support, such as counselling or therapy, can help process trauma and cope with stress. Many organizations offer services specifically tailored for refugees and immigrants.

Develop Coping Mechanism:
Engage in activities that alleviate stress, such as exercise, meditation, journaling, or engaging in hobbies you enjoy.

Maintain Optimism:
Focusing on small victories and positive aspects of your new environment can help maintain a hopeful outlook.

Stay Connected with Culture:
Preserving cultural practices, languages, and traditions can provide a sense of continuity and identity.

Building Social Networks

Find Community Groups:
Join expatriate or refugee organizations and community groups where you can connect with others who share similar experiences.

Build Relationships with Locals:
Establish genuine connections with people in the host country. Mutual respect and understanding can foster strong friendships.

Volunteer:
Helping others can build a sense of purpose and forge new social ties. It can also provide valuable experience and knowledge about the host community.

Practical Adaptation

Learn the Language:
Language proficiency significantly enhances your ability to integrate, secure employment, and access resources. Many communities offer free or low-cost language classes.

Understand Local Laws and Rights:
Familiarize yourself with the legal landscape of the host country, including your rights regarding work, residence, and social services.

Pursue Education and Training:

Enroll in courses or vocational training to enhance your skills and qualifications. This can improve employment prospects and provide a sense of achievement.

Find Suitable Employment:
Seek job placement programs or organizations that assist immigrants and refugees. Don't hesitate to take entry-level positions as a stepping stone to better opportunities.

Utilize Available Resources

Access Social Services:
Utilize the social services available, such as healthcare, housing assistance, and educational resources. Many NGOs and community organizations can assist in navigating these services.

Financial Planning:
Manage finances carefully, especially if resources are limited. Budgeting and, if possible, saving some money can provide a safety net.

Legal Aid:
Engage with legal aid organizations that can help you secure your legal status and protect your rights.

Engage in Civic Participation

Be Informed:
Stay updated on news and policies affecting immigrants and refugees. Understanding the political climate can help you anticipate changes and take action when necessary.

Advocacy:
Engage in advocacy efforts for refugee and immigrant rights. This can provide a sense of purpose and potentially improve conditions for yourself and others in

similar situations.

Participate in Community Life:
Attend local events, volunteer, and engage in civic activities. Active participation can foster a sense of belonging and contribute to the community.

Long-Term Planning

Set Goals:
Establish short-term and long-term objectives for your personal and professional life. Achieving these goals can give you a sense of direction and accomplishment.

Stay Hopeful for Reunification:
If separated from family, work towards family reunification, if possible, and maintain contact through calls, messaging apps, or social media.

Consider Future Options:
Stay open to new opportunities, whether it's settling permanently in the host country, returning home if conditions improve, or moving to another country with better prospects.

Enduring exile requires resilience, adaptability, and the ability to leverage available resources and networks. While the circumstances of exile can be daunting, fostering psychological resilience, building social support, adapting practically, and engaging in the community can significantly enhance one's ability to endure and thrive. With patience, persistence, and support, it is possible to rebuild one's life and find a sense of belonging and purpose in a new environment.

Life in exile has never been an easy thing. We try to comply with the systems of the country to bring us clarity in order for life to be more pleasant for us. One effort that most of us made appeared to be deemed a scandal by others. Places that we knew of, which could accommodate us, were the only ones where we could survive. We had to be accountable for the moves we made whilst every punch thrown at us was blocked and deflected.

How do we cope in exile?

Do people really cope in exile? If your answer is 'yes', why? How do they feel when they are unable to cope? This chapter gives answers to these questions, explaining what we face in exile. It is well known that life hasn't become easier from what we have heard on a daily basis.

My attention was focused. I knew things could have been easier to obtain. Instead, however, it took a negative direction. Nonetheless, when I tried to be positive, it seemed more difficult. I believe life with fellow brothers was in tune to mine. Because of what we felt during troubled times, the grievances we experienced were similar to those we had prior. Thus, we had no option but to endure them until they were dealt with. The most common understanding we shared was 'everything is allowed'.

Under these conditions, most people went on a negative route in their lives as coping was a battle and life wasn't easy. Others went to jail which was a common practice. The prison was even nicknamed a 'crèche' because, if one was incarcerated, they were treated like kids – staying in one place and given food. This kind of life was unappreciated by some of us because it was denigrating to a level of disrespect by the community. I can say that my task was to observe the whole scenario, what people had undergone, which gave me the courage to write about it. Thus, all things were quickly flashing past in my vision and most of what I found was people being victimised.

Life hadn't turned optimistically for us. We were found more often engulfed in the situations that were so challenging but we said nothing as that was a time to remain silent, merely because we were not native to that particular country. We had this name given to us, 'kwerekwere', which was derived from a dispersal regard.

The efforts we make in South Africa depend on our own ways of living, especially when using our own intelligence. Thus, we need to express it like this: *"We are running from the enemy after learning his tactics and how quickly the enemy moves. Therefore, we need to save our own lives and whoever is left behind will face pain and hardship"*.

Now, regarding life in South Africa, most people face impossible odds when danger looms bringing tremendous pressure to deal with.

It is so difficult to cope in exile.

There are so many things which people embraced that they shouldn't have. In certain situations, victimised people are hindered in performing according to their skills. We all tend to lose the image of being successful in life when we're found in terrible situations. From time to time, particularly when things become extremely unpleasant, some moments are perceived as an image of failure which brings self-condemnation.

Coping in exile is not an easy thing. Many times, when we make a serious move and call upon Almighty God, He comes to our aid. Are we really loved in times like this? When we're found in a difficult situation, are people there to help us? Love is seen in reciprocal way in South Africa.

If one doesn't have what someone needs, sometimes situations don't result in peace and this is mostly in Black environments. According to my research, I have discovered that poverty within the Black population has made many use flattery to hide their motives. The most vulnerable people herein have always been immigrants who have endured all sorts of insults which includes those who went to Home

Affairs. This was very discouraging and disappointing to witness immigrants being so rudely treated.

Whilst I was writing this book, it seemed that every experience and event around me challenged my zeal. I battled with many things in order to successfully write this book. For many years, I experienced different challenges but I had the courage to progress through it.

- I battled to focus because my *fiancé* had greatly disappointed me.
- I had respected her culture by paying what had been required of me regarding dowry.
- I had placed much confidence in her but she left me.
- I also lost my job during that time and ridiculously began to condemn my entire life in South Africa.

In my highly emotional state, I believed that everything had been in vain. I seemed to be in a vacuum. I couldn't see myself coping and my hope began to diminish. Then I saw a way open and in it I found myself carrying the burden of humiliation. As I walked that way, I approached a certain place where people were uncouth.

I was unsure of that small way wherein these uncouth people who, when they saw my determination, started giving me a hard time. This deeply disturbed and discouraged me. Despite this trouble, I was determined to move on. I knew the only way to conquer was to keep going.

Many times, we do take negative routes because of the gravity of trouble and some of us battle to overcome. What do we really deserve when we're not in our native countries? I believe that, above all, we deserve respect when we serve others. I can also say that we are gracious people in all circumstances. We do not count the cost or question our ability to cope but, with self-determination, we brilliantly move on in a manner that shows respect to others. When we adopt this attitude, it encourages us to keep improving in our quest to better ourselves.

Life on one's own in exile is never easy. However, we all strive to be conquerors. We aimed to survive in the situation previously taking place with systems implemented by those seen as leaders of the world. I am deeply emphasising all the pain we undergo which isn't accommodated by anyone. This is accepted by most of those found in exile who have no other alternative.

Those of us in South Africa who are in exile differ from one another in many ways. Although we come from different backgrounds as well as countries, we are all on the same ground.

Chapter 8

Religious beliefs in exile

I often ask myself these questions:
- Why do we have religion?
- Do humans need religion?
- Does it have anything to do with life?

Religion often plays a significant and multifaceted role in the life of individuals in exile. For many refugees and immigrants, religious beliefs and practices can provide a source of comfort, community, and identity the upheaval and uncertainty of exile. Here's a closer look at how religious beliefs can impact and shape the experience of individuals in exile:

Sources of Comfort and Hope

Spiritual Refuge:
Religious beliefs can offer emotional solace and a sense of spiritual refuge. Many find strength and hope through prayer, meditation, and other religious practices, which can help them cope with the trauma and stress of displacement.

Meaning and Purpose:
Religion can provide a framework for understanding suffering and hardship. Beliefs in a higher purpose or divine plan can instill a sense of meaning amidst adversity.

Rituals and Traditions:
Maintaining religious rituals and traditions can offer a

comforting sense of continuity and normalcy in an otherwise disorienting experience. These practices can help preserve a sense of identity and cultural heritage.

Building Community and Social Support

Faith Communities:
Religious institutions and congregations often provide vital support networks for immigrants and refugees. Places of worship can become centers of social activity, offering community, friendship, and practical assistance.

Mutual Support:
Within faith communities, individuals can find mutual aid and support, such as shared resources, communal meals, and help with housing, employment, and other necessities.

Interfaith Solidarity:
Religious organizations sometimes engage in interfaith initiatives, promoting solidarity and cooperation among diverse faith groups. This can enhance social cohesion and support for refugees and immigrants.

Practical Assistance and Advocacy

Charitable Services:
Many religious organizations run charities and aid programs providing essential services like food, shelter, healthcare, and legal assistance to refugees and immigrants.

Advocacy and Rights:
Religious leaders and institutions may also engage in advocacy efforts, campaigning for refugee and immigrant rights, and working to influence public policy in favor of more compassionate and inclusive measures.

Challenges and Considerations

Religious Freedom:

In some host countries, refugees and immigrants might face restrictions on religious practices or discrimination based on their faith. It's crucial to understand the local context and find ways to practice one's faith safely.

Interfaith Relations:
Navigating a multi-religious society can present challenges, but it also offers opportunities for interfaith dialogue and understanding. Respecting and learning about other faith traditions can enhance mutual respect and integration.

Identity and Integration:
Balancing the preservation of religious identity with the need to integrate into the host society can be complex. Finding a harmonious way to practice and express one's faith while embracing aspects of the new culture is key.

Personal Growth and Resilience

Faith-Driven Resilience:
Religious beliefs can foster resilience by providing a sense of hope and the strength to persevere. Many find that their faith helps them to endure hardships with greater fortitude and optimism.

Moral and Ethical Guidance:
Religion often offers moral and ethical frameworks that guide behavior and decision-making. This guidance can be especially valuable in navigating the complexities and challenges of exile.

Renewed Faith:
For some, the experience of exile can lead to a deepening or transformation of faith. The challenges faced may prompt a renewed spirituality or a more profound sense of religious commitment.

Religion can be a vital source of comfort, strength, and community for individuals in exile. It offers emotional solace, practical support, and a sense of identity and purpose. Engaging with religious communities can provide critical resources and advocacy. However, refugees and immigrants must navigate these opportunities while being mindful of potential challenges, such as religious discrimination or the need for interfaith understanding. By integrating their faith into their new lives, many people in exile find the resilience and support they need to overcome adversity and build a hopeful future.

When I thought about this more deeply, I became curious, wanting to know what religion was about and, if it existed, what the essentials were.

Some say they don't see why we get involved in religion. Others say it's better to get involved when they are much older. There are even those who don't want to hear of it. These questions can create confusion and most of these people don't get answers. However, this chapter may respond to some of your questions which you may have been asking for so long without answers.

If we think of some of these questions that were asked in the previous chapter, I offer an understanding concerning our ancestors. It is well known that this was a concept which our forefathers had in their beliefs concerning worshipping their ancestors.

The point is that different concepts we have from various religions have contributed to an understanding of where we are dealing with cultural differences. These should be shared with those who amass the African traditions without limitations to common religions which are well known.

Religion is very important to those who are in exile. Thus, through religion, we get to exercise our faith as well as expressing our religious identity. This is needed in all sectors of life in the same way that our forefathers needed their ancestors.

As the writer of this book, I personally believed religion wasn't so important, though I found myself in a Christian family and pretended to be one of the siblings who were devoted believers. However, the fear of my parents, who were very committed to Christianity, wouldn't allow me to live the way I wanted to.

Somehow, my father could tell I was pretending. That was when he frequently used proverbs to show me that I wasn't a sincere Christian. I share this story with you in order to make you aware of what we do sometimes, thinking that it produces good fruit in our lives. Yet, in some way, we face the reality that we've been running from. I came to see the importance of religion when I found myself on my own with nobody on my side. It was during my times of trouble that I knew my only friend was God. That's when those whom I considered my best friends had forsaken me because they couldn't bear with me during my troubles.

This is the only time in my entire life I learnt that running to God was the best for me. In addition to this, I finally committed to a certain religion which helped me have some strategies in seeking God until I accepted that my first priority in life should be Him.

In South Africa, there are many people who have different beliefs and religions such as Christianity, Hinduism, Islam, Buddhism, Shembe and many more. Each individual feels so comfortable worshipping in the religion they prefer. However, there are those involved in some of these religions for the sake of being breadwinners.

Certain challenges, which some experience daily, don't offer anything that will define them. Rather than being benefitted spiritually, they only receive according to their physical desires. There are others who are used by some of the leaders of these religions. In certain religions, there are many benefits offered, particularly to needy people such as refugees and others who are found in positions wherein they can't help themselves either physically or spiritually.

Let us look at the crisis which took place in Zimbabwe due to economic and political problems caused by the greed of those seen as leaders. I've heard there are many who have moved from Zimbabwe to South Africa, Swaziland, Botswana and Mozambique. Most of these people are accommodated by the Church – assistance that cannot be provided by any other group, company or organisation. However, without appearing as materialists toward religion, we can also look at some spiritual advantages for those who affiliate themselves with religion in terms of practising love and having heartfelt compassion toward those who are seen in destitution.

There is a spirit of confraternity in some of the religions which has been seen as great concern regarding those who reliably devote themselves. For this reason, I rise up again by saying that those in South Africa and elsewhere around the world should consider that many times, when we are found to be conquerors, it's not by our mighty power or abilities but by the grace of our God. However, among those who take time to read my book, some may not like this chapter if they don't believe in God, the Creator. Nevertheless, if you aren't interested in the chapter, know this – as one found in exile, I've seen the importance of believing in God. You should once again know that *God is the Creator* of the universe which includes earth and mankind.

We shouldn't come up with a type of philosophy that is full of causality, trying to find out about His existence and being. All we must focus on is that He was, He is and He forever shall be.

The way we perceive life in exile is different from others because, on our side, everything is difficult to obtain. There are times when we long to be considered to some point but we find it impossible from where we are.

When we trust God, things happen automatically and that's when He becomes the first priority in our lives. You may not conceive this if you don't use a certain metaphor which can at least allow you to come to a realisation concerning this chapter as far as God's intervention toward mankind is concerned.

At this point so far, I cannot specify that this is good for everyone, not only us who are in exile, but even those who are known as natives of a particular place. With all the advantages we do have in life, even living outside our countries, mostly, if we encounter religions similar to ours, religious people are at times kind to those who are of the same faith and, if not, they aren't considered by people from other religions.

This chapter doesn't necessarily show only a positive side, but also a negative one. This is well seen by those who have been spectators of what occurred around them. The disadvantages are seen in the form of hatred and competition which lies in the reciprocal scenario which is, *"I'll help you if you are of my faith"*. In addition to this, there are other things a person may say, such as how much good they do and how far they've come. That's why many people involve themselves in religions we're not supposed to follow and this is exactly what causes people to criticise religion. However, even though some religious views differ, reflecting good and bad, I cannot hide my feelings concerning them.

Thus, this is one of the known channels that will cause the seepage of evil into the Church of God. You may not agree with me on this point, but I tell you this – *be aware of what is taking place in the world today.*

Politically, we find that religions are much more involved. Economically, we can also see the complaint concerning some religions – that the people are too quick to express their concerns and are willing to come up with certain solutions that will play to the satisfaction of the world.

How many religious leaders are seen getting involved in world organisations, using motives that are attached to the

Church to be uplifting, when we know quite well that the cornerstone of the Church is Jesus. All we need to do is stand as watchmen because, one way or another, people will move on with deceitful beliefs.

The Church and religious minds are where we find help and love. These are now being counterfeited from genuine love and help, which are obviously used by many religious leaders found in the same community in order to provide one of these two things.

With my attributes given on previous pages regarding church hospitality, you may view me as speaking generally without any exception. However, there is an exception herein derived from an experience I had eight years ago. That is why, on this point, I cannot generalise that much, having experienced hospitality in Mozambique. I well recall the way I had been welcomed by one of the Roman Catholic churches through their hospitality. There was no discrimination against me even though I'd mentioned that I had come from the Protestant faith.

There were other places I went to such as Tanzania. As I was uninvolved in their religion, they couldn't provide any help at all as far as accommodation was concerned.

Chapter 9

The choices we make in exile

Living in exile presents a unique set of challenges and opportunities, compelling individuals to make choices that significantly affect their present circumstances and future prospects. These decisions can range from practical considerations such as housing and employment to deeper existential choices about identity, community, and ethos. Here are some key choices that individuals may face in exile and the implications of these decisions:

Choosing the Right Location

Asylum or Host Country:
The choice of where to seek asylum or settle can significantly impact your experience in exile. Factors such as the country's political climate, economic opportunities, social services, and existing diasporic communities should be considered.

Urban vs. Rural:
Deciding whether to live in an urban or rural setting can affect access to jobs, social services, and community support.

Legal and Documentation Choices

Asylum Applications:
Navigating the asylum process requires understanding

legal requirements and often seeking legal assistance. The outcome of your application can impact your ability to stay in a country and access services.

Document Maintenance:
Keeping your documents safe and up to date is crucial. This includes birth certificates, educational qualifications, and any refugee status documentation.

Employment and Education

Job Market:
Deciding whether to take up immediate work that may be unrelated to your skills, or to pursue further education or retraining, can shape your economic future.

Skill Development:
Investing in learning the language of the host country, gaining new skills, or furthering your education can offer better employment opportunities and integration prospects.

Health and Well-being

Healthcare Access:
Understanding and navigating the healthcare system in your host country is essential. Prioritizing mental health services can also play a crucial role in coping with the trauma of displacement.

Self-Care:
Developing routines and practices that support your physical and emotional well-being, such as exercise, proper nutrition, and hobbies, can significantly improve your quality of life.

Community and Social Connections

Building Networks:
Actively seeking to build a supportive social network

can help mitigate the feelings of isolation that often accompany exile. This network can include fellow exiles, locals, and members of faith communities.

Cultural Integration vs Preservation:
Balancing the preservation of your cultural identity with the need to integrate into the host society is a delicate yet vital choice. Engaging in both can foster a richer, more inclusive community.

Personal and Family Decisions

Family Reunification:
If separated from your family, deciding whether and how to pursue family reunification should be a priority. This can often involve complex legal processes.

Educational Decisions for Children:
Ensuring your children have access to education and opportunities is crucial for their integration and future success.

Political Engagement and Advocacy

Activism:
Deciding whether to engage in political activism, either related to your home country or refugee rights in your host country, can be empowering but also risky.

Staying Informed:
Keeping abreast of changes in immigration laws and policies can help you make informed decisions about your future.

Financial Choices

Budgeting:
Managing your finances carefully is crucial, especially if resources are limited. Developing a budget and sticking to it can provide some financial stability.

Savings and Investments:
If possible, saving money or investing in education and skills can provide a safety net and improve future prospects.

Religious and Ethical Choices

Faith Community Engagement: Choosing to engage with faith communities can offer emotional support, moral guidance, and practical assistance.

Ethical Living:
Upholding your ethical and moral values, even in challenging circumstances, can provide a sense of integrity and purpose.

Long-Term Planning

Future Residency:
Making decisions about whether to stay permanently in your host country, return to your homeland if conditions improve, or move to another country with better prospects.

Goal Setting:
Setting short-term and long-term goals can provide direction and a sense of purpose. These goals can range from personal development to career aspirations to community involvement.

The choices made in exile are complex and multifaceted, affecting both the immediate quality of life and long-term prospects. These decisions often require careful consideration, resilience, and resourcefulness. While the challenges are significant, thoughtful choices can lead to personal growth, community integration, and a sense of purpose. In navigating these decisions, leveraging available resources, seeking support, and maintaining hope and determination can help build a more secure and fulfilling life in exile.

Fulfilling life in exile requires resilience, adaptability, and the pursuit of emotional, social, and financial well-being despite the challenges. Here are some strategies and practices to help make life in exile more fulfilling:

Establishing Stability and Security

Legal and Financial Stability

Legal Assistance: Seek legal advice to understand your rights and obligations in the host country. Apply for asylum or legal residency where possible to secure your legal status.

Financial Planning:
Develop a budget and financial plan to manage resources effectively. Seek employment, even if it's temporary or part-time, and explore microfinancing or small business opportunities.

Safe Housing

Secure Accommodation:
Find safe and stable housing. Connect with local non-profits or government programs that offer housing assistance for refugees or exiles.

Create a Home:
Make your living space comfortable and personal. Even small touches can make a significant difference in how connected and secure you feel.

Building a Support Network

Community Involvement

Join Community Groups:
Connect with local ethnic, cultural, or religious communities that offer support and a sense of belonging.

Many communities have organizations specifically to help newcomers integrate.

Volunteer Work:
Volunteering can provide a sense of purpose, help you meet new people, and integrate into your new community.

Social Connections

Build Relationships:
Form friendships and relationships with both fellow exiles and local residents. Social connections are vital for emotional support and can help ease the feelings of isolation.

Family Reunification:
If possible, work on legal and logistical means to reunite with family members. Strong family support is crucial for well-being.

Focusing on Well-being

Mental and Emotional Health

Seek Counselling:
Many organizations offer free or low-cost counselling services for exiles. Talking to a mental health professional can help process trauma, stress, and other emotional challenges.

Practice Self-care:
Engage in activities that promote mental well-being, such as meditation, exercise, or creative pursuits like art and music.

Physical Health

Access Healthcare:
Utilize local healthcare services, NGOs, or international organizations that provide medical care to displaced

individuals. Regular checkups and treatment are essential.

Healthy Lifestyle:
Maintain a balanced diet and regular physical activity to remain healthy and mitigate stress.

Education and Skill Development

Learning the Language

Language Classes:
Enroll in language courses to improve your proficiency in the host country's language. This can facilitate social integration and improve employment prospects.

Practice Regularly:
Use language-learning apps, engage in conversations with native speakers, and read local newspapers or watch local TV shows.

Furthering Education

Continue Education:
Look for opportunities to continue your education, whether through formal institutions, online courses, or certifications. Many countries offer scholarships or financial aid for refugees.

Skill Development:
Learn new skills or improve existing ones through vocational training, workshops, or community education programs.

Employment and Economic Empowerment

Job Search

Employment Assistance Programs:
Utilize employment services and programs that assist exiled individuals in finding jobs, such as NGOs

specializing in workforce reintegration.

Networking:
Attend job fairs, networking events, and get involved in community activities to increase job opportunities.

Entrepreneurship

Start a Business:
Consider starting a small business if permitted. This not only provides financial stability but also a sense of purpose and achievement.

Microloans and Grants:
Seek out microloans, grants, or funding opportunities specifically designed for refugees and displaced persons.

Maintaining Cultural Identity

Cultural Practices

Celebrate Traditions:
Keep cultural and religious traditions alive through celebrations, rituals, and customs. This provides a sense of continuity and stability.

Share Culture:
Share your culture with local communities through food, art, music, and stories. This can build bridges and foster mutual respect and understanding.

Cultural Organizations

Join Cultural Groups:
Participate in cultural organizations or clubs that reflect your heritage. These groups can provide emotional support and maintain your cultural identity.

Setting and Pursuing Goals

Short-term and Long-term Goals

Set Achievable Goals:
Define clear, realistic short-term and long-term goals. This could include personal, educational, or professional objectives.

Monitor Progress:
Regularly check your progress towards these goals. Adjust them as necessary to stay motivated and focused.

Celebrating Milestones

Acknowledge Achievements:
Celebrate your achievements, no matter how small. Recognizing progress and successes can boost morale and motivation.

This chapter is an essential story concerning those together in exile in a sense of reproach to some things relating to hatred which comes from the natives of the country. The chapter will explain the disadvantages that we experience in our daily lives in South Africa.

Life is unfair on our side. We try by all means to get the zeal we envisaged to have a life which gives us hope for the future. I'm very vocal in this chapter as far as my questions are concerned, being all about the things we pursue which tend to be unavailable due to certain issues.

My concerns are so specific in different areas, causing numerous gaps between us and our fellow brothers who are maltreating others for reasons that are so banal. At this point in time, my courage failed me, leaving me no choice but to exit the country.

Xenophobic attacks started while I was preparing to marry a South African girl, whereas the natives of South Africa were accusing foreigners of taking their women from them. But what amazed me in the whole scenario was that the perpetrators seemed to be some who were seen as leaders in South Africa, knowing the value of humanitarians, who also felt the pressure of life in exile.

On this point, we can afford to blame those who are seen as xenophobic actors but we cannot see those who are playing it behind closed doors. This is the complaint of those who hear victims asking questions such as:

- *'Where shall we go?'*
- *'Where should we run?'*
- *'Is there any place to hide?'*

This is a very difficult time whereby everyone lives with tension because of the situation regarding killings and beatings without choosing who is legal and who is not. It is a bad time even to those who came for tourism in South Africa.

South Africa has lost its attraction due to its reputation and hostility to foreigners. It's time for people to become vigilant regarding the atrocity taking place among the natives in the country. Personally, as the author of this book, I'm in South Africa as a student and in a dilemma as to what I should do. What choice should we make when our human rights are taken away? How can people survive amid hatred demonstrated toward foreigners, sharing the same continent? This is one of the most difficult times I have experienced during the period I've spent outside of my own country.

I cannot remember all the times which have been tough on me, but my comments throughout this chapter emphasise the pain we feel as we are not familiar with these types of situations. However, we don't have a choice as we are surrounded with situations we cannot afford to be in.

Choices are made individually but the outcomes thereof

always seem to generally reflect the environment around us, whether positively or negatively. We each have our own choices to make because, many times when we make choices, they are for our own benefit. However, in the life we live today, there are many who don't know what to do or what choices to make. They are just as empty and some of these are caused by confusion they come across in life. They finally start to blame those around them.

There are times when our choices tend to become obstacles. When we make them at an inappropriate time or place or with negative people, that's when we tend to blame the world because we submit to our fleshly desires which hinder us from choosing wisely. I've met many who were refugees in South Africa including doctors with qualifications they obtained in their own countries. Some of these people were jobless. I asked some of them why they held such qualifications without using them rather than guarding cars. They replied they didn't have a choice. That was one of the reasons why they ended up as car guards. There were also others who were ministers, seen as politicians from their native countries, becoming security officers while they were in exile.

Such circumstances in life don't really define the future even though we're so often nervous of this type of situation. Even those around us think it's over for us. That's when they show pity, judging in their small minds, believing we won't cope. They have distantly viewed us, without realising no-one knows what tomorrow will bring. We may not have a choice today, but tomorrow our choices could seal our future. People may judge us with a naked eye, only to understand later they were promoting us from a hidden view to an open one. In other words, from nothing to something. Many times, our choices, whether positive or negative, have been guided by our feelings rather than our abilities. However, the life choices we make outside our native countries are mostly dominated by fear.

Earlier, I explained how it feels to be trapped in situations whereby everything seems on top of us. If we don't pay attention, some of us may end up sleeping in the open through making choices according to our own desires. However, those who respect the rhythm of exile do survive and tend to conquer because they first put on the garment of humility which is a great weapon for success in everything.

Some people chose to end their lives because of certain situations they believed they couldn't handle, which operated negatively in their lives, bringing a negative outlook of their futures. These people couldn't see any other option but to destroy their souls without calling on God. How about those who choose to do evil due to situations that influence them? The world itself is not cruel but many people in it are. We often blame the world, forgetting that it consists of the people living in it. This is not only for those in exile but also for those who are not, particularly whoever reads this book.

When I looked at the consequences of negative, irreversible choices, these led to regret and questions such as:

- *'Was I out of my mind?'*
- *'How could I do this?'*

We try to introspect when it's too late. Even when we can't choose what we want because of limitations caused by the country's structures, we should know that, no matter how isolated we may be, it doesn't mean we should lose our sense of choice. If we do, we may regret it.

It is well known that most of our brothers are drug dealers. Their excuse is they don't have a choice because they aren't given the chance to find better employment. Some of our brothers believe there is no other option but dealing in matters that destroy the lives of others. Although they know it's illegal, they keep doing it. We know choices are made individually which can be done emotionally or psychologically. However, when we know the choice we've made is destructive, we try to rectify what we did in that emotional state and then blame those around us. Choice should be something we pay attention to before we make it as we know the future lies in the choices made, thoughtfully or otherwise.

There are those who die from various illnesses who have no control over them. We should bear in mind that the choice we make determines our future, so be careful what choice you make in life. You may ruin your entire future by making a rash or unwise choice.

Today, there are various illnesses such as diabetes, cancer, TB and others which can kill rapidly. However, in the following chapter, I'll be talking specifically about HIV / AIDS and show that numerous people chose to embrace it as they had no control over the way they felt at that point in time.

I cannot generalise when it comes to those who were infected with venereal disease. Some people are infected by their partners and others through accidents (blood transfusion etc.). Innocent children get contaminated through their parents' actions who may not know much about life, so on this point I'll be specific on what causes problems with individuals.

Chapter **10**

The issue of HIV / AIDS in exile

The issue of HIV/AIDS in exile is a multifaceted challenge that intersects with health, social, legal, and human rights domains. Refugees, internally displaced persons (IDPs), and often face increased vulnerabilities and barriers in accessing HIV prevention, treatment, and care services. Here an in-depth look at the complexities and considerations surrounding HIV/AIDS in exile:

Increased Vulnerability to HIV/AIDS

Disrupted Healthcare Services:
Displacement often leads to disrupted healthcare systems, making it difficult for those living with HIV to access consistent treatment and care.

Exposure to Risk Factors:
Conditions of displacement, such as overcrowded camps, lack of protection, and economic instability, can increase exposure to risk factors like sexual violence, transactional sex, and limited access to preventive measures (e.g., condoms, clean needles).

Stigma and Discrimination:
HIV/AIDS-related stigma and discrimination can be exacerbated in displacement settings, where social cohesion may be weakened, and misinformation can spread easily.

Mental Health:
The trauma and stress of displacement can negatively impact mental health, which in turn can affect one's ability to practice safe behaviors and adhere to treatment regimens.

Barriers to Prevention, Treatment, and Care

Limited Healthcare Infrastructure:
Refugee camps and host communities often have inadequate healthcare infrastructure, which can hinder the provision of HIV/AIDS services.

Legal and Policy Barriers:
Refugees and migrants may face legal obstacles that limit their access to healthcare. This can include restrictive immigration policies, lack of legal status, and exclusion from national health programs.

Language and Cultural Barriers:
Language differences and cultural misunderstandings between healthcare providers and displaced individuals can impede effective communication and care.

Financial Constraints:
Poverty and lack of resources among displaced populations can limit access to healthcare services and necessary medications.

Addressing HIV/AIDS in Exile

Prevention

Education and Awareness:
Implementing culturally sensitive education programs about HIV prevention is crucial. These programs should address myths, encourage testing, and promote safe practices.

Access to Preventive Measures:

Ensuring the availability of condoms, clean needles, and other preventive tools is essential. Programs should also include pre-exposure prophylaxis (PrEP) and post-exposure prophylaxis (PEP).

Protection Mechanisms:
Strengthening protection mechanisms in camps and displacement settings can mitigate exposure to violence and exploitation, reducing the risk of HIV transmission.

Treatment and Care

Integration of Services:
HIV services should be integrated into primary health care to ensure accessibility and sustainability. This includes routine testing, antiretroviral therapy (ART), and the management of opportunistic infections.

Mobile and Outreach Clinics:
Mobile health units and outreach programs can provide crucial services to those who cannot easily access fixed healthcare facilities.

Mental Health Support:
Providing mental health and psychosocial support is vital for individuals living with HIV, helping them cope with the stress of displacement and the disease.

Legal and Policy Support

Inclusive Policies:
Advocacy for inclusive policies that ensure refugees and migrants can access healthcare services without discrimination is crucial.

Legal Aid:
Providing legal assistance to help displaced individuals navigate the legal system and secure their rights to

healthcare is beneficial.

Community Involvement

Community Leaders and Peer Educators:
Engaging community leaders and training peer educators can enhance the reach and effectiveness of prevention and care programs.

Support Groups:
Establishing support groups for people living with HIV can provide emotional support, encourage adherence to treatment, and reduce stigma.

Role of International Organizations

United Nations and NGOs:
Organizations like UNHCR, WHO, and various NGOs play a critical role in addressing HIV/AIDS in displacement settings. They can provide funding, technical support, and implement programs tailored to the needs of displaced populations.

Coordination and Collaboration:
Effective coordination between humanitarian organizations, host governments, and local communities is essential for the successful implementation of HIV/AIDS interventions.

HIV/AIDS presents significant challenges for displaced populations, but with coordinated efforts, these challenges can be addressed effectively. Prevention, treatment, and care must be integrated into the broader humanitarian response, with a focus on accessibility, inclusivity, and cultural sensitivity. By leveraging the strengths of international organizations, local communities, and healthcare systems, it is possible to mitigate the impact of HIV/AIDS among those in exile and improve their quality of life.

The main concept of this chapter is based on a psychological reproach toward AIDS as being an exterminator of people. There are millions who have been vulnerably taken away by this horrible disease. Research has been done even up to this moment you're reading this book. There are those who tirelessly search for a remedy for this disease. Some say it's a punishment from God brought upon mankind because of their weakness. There has been much debate regarding this disease and more suspicions regarding it. However, some things that have been said about AIDS are uncertain as one doesn't reach an answer that will help communities.

If we ignore the implementation of self-discipline, we will remain ignorant, thus endangering our own lives and those we love and with whom we share the planet. What about our children? My aim in this chapter is to remind you of your precious life. You should be more responsible, bearing in mind the best control over your life depends only on you.

Regarding HIV / AIDS, I'll address what I understand about how most people become infected with the virus. Again, I'll be more realistic regarding things that hook most people in exile. I'll be specific about the reality of our brothers who are taking life for granted by not taking precautions which could result in endangering their daily lives. Whether we are in exile or not, it's a matter we all need to concentrate on in order to live a long life.

Some people don't want to touch on points like this even though they know it's a matter of life and death. We all want to live without any sort of sickness or problem relating to health. This chapter is very relevant and it is for you, the reader, to conduct yourself in a beneficial way regarding health as well as choosing wisely as opposed to those who lose control of their lives.

The issue of HIV / AIDS has become a serious matter, having taken millions of lives – plus there are those on treatment who don't know what tomorrow holds for them. It is very difficult to act 'happy' when 'sorrow' knocks on our door unexpectedly. There has to be a subconscious change that takes place which will occur in your senses, impacting your innermost man. There are many opinions regarding this incurable disease, yet people still can't figure out how to deal with it.

Although researchers have tried their best to find an answer regarding the disease, their information is still uncertain – mere estimations. Why don't people call on God, the Creator of Heaven and Earth for the answers?

HIV / AIDS is a disease which attacks your immune system, irrespective of colour, beauty or title. It kills mercilessly.

It is very difficult to share the truth with people when they choose to live in ignorance. The number of those who left this world through this terrible disease is tragic. Some who had already died (now in the afterlife) came to realise that it is better to preserve life. Thus, their souls now regret that there is no way back to this life to reverse anything.

It is important to heed that, when we give in to weakness, we have only ourselves to blame. We have life in abundance. Why should we give it up when we can preserve it? This doesn't concern only those who are in exile. Every individual needs to learn the value of life. Most of those in exile have been pushed by economic change or political regime and war.

After reaching South Africa, those in exile complain of their fear of life. Others even state they ran from war and political and economic change, now facing the big crisis of HIV / AIDS. My comment on this was that people who said this were very concerned about life, leaving their beautiful countries and facing this type of crises found in South Africa. HIV / AIDS is also found in many other countries.

In addition to this, there are other issues relating to xenophobia found in autochthones of this country. *Isn't this dangerous?* Thus, we are still unsure of what comes next – what the future holds. We need to focus on what the whole world longs for. Nobody in his right mind has ever longed for death. However, there was one man named Bushero whom I read about whilst in high school. What was said about him interested me. He found life to be so difficult, he couldn't see any other option but death. His burden and difficulties were so severe, he ended his life. The story contained pictures which showed how traumatic his situation was.

When death came knocking, it came without notice, out of the darkness. When he saw that death was stalking him, he negotiated with death to not take him. To suffer and to die is part of the human cycle as no one will escape death. There have been many people who lost their lives from this 'exterminator' disease, that we have now had to bury. They didn't deserve it either but they were taken unexpectedly. We should deeply consider this as a problem so we can come up with a viable solution to overcome it.

Why should people suffer on this earth? Philosophically, we are 'the world' and it consists of the people who are living in it. That is why it is called 'the world'.

There is a significant point when people and the world collide, where your imagination runs wild. This can come from unexpected ideas and thoughts. When this is happens, it immediately links one to a new world where you tend to forget where you are standing on the earth, while being part of another world.

In the world system, there is much trouble with sicknesses, stress, injustice and much more. All these attack the inhabitants of the earth – mankind. I am very concerned about what's going on in the current situation surrounding us. I have many questions and I'm curious to know what's really involved concerning HIV / AIDS.

There is so much speculation over it. Is it true that it's because of poverty? What they say about it is not 100%

true. There hasn't been any scientific solution. There has been much speculation as to where in the body it's found but they haven't found a cure for it. Many books have been published about HIV / AIDS. The media have been involved in the search for a solution but have been unsuccessful. We see how HIV / AIDS is destroying people yet some people don't think it will happen to them. When it knocks on their doors, then they will experience the consequence of their actions. What does one's ancestors say about that?

One day, I walked to the beach deep in thought. I felt very burdened about there being no solution to this disease. I thought no-one else had a problem that was bigger than mine. Whilst walking, I came across a young girl whose life was in a chaotic state. She looked weak, facing the ocean. I went to her. As I walked closer, she could sense my movement. She looked very sad. I looked her directly in the eyes and greeted her. I began to speak to see if she was willing to talk to me. She responded positively without any indication that she had a problem. I asked why the water looked green. She said it may be because it was summer. We immediately switched to issues of life.

My purpose in approaching this girl was to find relief from my disappointment, which I had encountered previously, making it difficult for me to relate to people. I needed reassurance that could come from speaking to someone, particularly one who had experienced something similar to what I had.

I feel so relieved when I speak to someone about issues which overwhelm me. We all need such types of people to bring us a sense of self-worth. Many times, when we're in a situation, the first thing we long for is peace of mind. We often see people, particularly those infected with the HIV virus, having a psychological breakdown.

Without any notification, their status may change, so when they find themselves in a position where sickness overtakes them, they could panic or experience doubts and fears. It was so sad to hear this from several people who were found in this manner where, at first, they couldn't find anything suitable to assist them medically or physically.

They were still healthy as far as their status was concerned but, when they received the diagnosis report, that was when things went downhill. They began to lose interest in living. Depression and fear stepped in, possibly causing them to end their lives. However, we do remember some things in our lives that enable us to look to the future and make us proud, keeping us from making any bad decisions. Whenever we decide on a poor choice for our life, we forget there is a solution. When we turn to God and trust Him, He can turn any situation we have into a solution. Therefore, we should take enough time to think about what happens after death.

We should keep in mind that there is a judgment to face for purposely ending our life. We must realise that being in this particular crisis does not mean life is over. We still have potential in the community.

Your employers still need you. They aren't concerned about your status. They care about your performance at work. Do not think negatively whereby you start limiting yourself by undermining your ability, thus setting yourself up to fail. This is about preventing your situation from overtaking you. Try to master your feelings toward this in a positive way. That's when you'll rise with renewed strength, overcoming all fear and thoughts that bring you down. The help you need is to find someone reliable to talk to who will be able to understand your situation, assisting you with advice that will give you peace of mind.

This is what we all long for. Whether the situation is good or bad, we need to find peace of mind. Sharing with our neighbour, friend or relative can give us some relief. We long to experience a normal status. This is how we feel as we remain in the struggle. When we overcome fear, depression and stress, we are much more inclined to succeed in spite of the negative report concerning our life.

We have more to face whilst living in this world, because, if we view things in the global sense, we discover that there are a lot of challenges to be faced whether we like it or not. Economic challenges can indicate life's standard, causing the poor to be destitute Whether we are rich or poor, we all face the same challenges and the economic crisis affects both groups, as emphasised in *Chapter 11*. Please pay attention to it.

The challenges we faced in exile

The issue of HIV/AIDS in exile is a multifaceted challenge that intersects with health, social, legal, and human rights domains. Refugees, internally displaced persons (IDPs), and often face increased vulnerabilities and barriers in accessing HIV prevention, treatment, and care services. Here an in-depth look at the complexities and considerations surrounding HIV/AIDS in exile:

Increased Vulnerability to HIV/AIDS

Disrupted Healthcare Services:
Displacement often leads to disrupted healthcare systems, making it difficult for those living with HIV to access consistent treatment and care.

Exposure to Risk Factors:
Conditions of displacement, such as overcrowded camps, lack of protection, and economic instability, can increase exposure to risk factors like sexual violence, transactional sex, and limited access to preventive measures (e.g., condoms, clean needles).

Stigma and Discrimination:
HIV/AIDS-related stigma and discrimination can be exacerbated in displacement settings, where social cohesion may be weakened, and misinformation can

spread easily.

Mental Health:
The trauma and stress of displacement can negatively impact mental health, which in turn can affect one's ability to practice safe behaviors and adhere to treatment regimens.

Barriers to Prevention, Treatment, and Care

Limited Healthcare Infrastructure:
Refugee camps and host communities often have inadequate healthcare infrastructure, which can hinder the provision of HIV/AIDS services.

Legal and Policy Barriers:
Refugees and migrants may face legal obstacles that limit their access to healthcare. This can include restrictive immigration policies, lack of legal status, and exclusion from national health programs.

Language and Cultural Barriers:
Language differences and cultural misunderstandings between healthcare providers and displaced individuals can impede effective communication and care.

Financial Constraints:
Poverty and lack of resources among displaced populations can limit access to healthcare services and necessary medications.

Addressing HIV/AIDS in Exile

Prevention

Education and Awareness:
Implementing culturally sensitive education programs about HIV prevention is crucial. These programs should address myths, encourage testing, and promote safe practices.

Access to Preventive Measures:
Ensuring the availability of condoms, clean needles, and other preventive tools is essential. Programs should also include pre-exposure prophylaxis (PrEP) and post-exposure prophylaxis (PEP).

Protection Mechanisms:
Strengthening protection mechanisms in camps and displacement settings can mitigate exposure to violence and exploitation, reducing the risk of HIV transmission.

Treatment and Care

Integration of Services:
HIV services should be integrated into primary health care to ensure accessibility and sustainability. This includes routine testing, antiretroviral therapy (ART), and the management of opportunistic infections.

Mobile and Outreach Clinics:
Mobile health units and outreach programs can provide crucial services to those who cannot easily access fixed healthcare facilities.

Mental Health Support:
Providing mental health and psychosocial support is vital for individuals living with HIV, helping them cope with the stress of displacement and the disease.

Legal and Policy Support

Inclusive Policies:
Advocacy for inclusive policies that ensure refugees and migrants can access healthcare services without discrimination is crucial.

Legal Aid:
Providing legal assistance to help displaced individuals

navigate the legal system and secure their rights to healthcare is beneficial.

Community Involvement

Community Leaders and Peer Educators:
Engaging community leaders and training peer educators can enhance the reach and effectiveness of prevention and care programs.

Support Groups:
Establishing support groups for people living with HIV can provide emotional support, encourage adherence to treatment, and reduce stigma.

Role of International Organizations

United Nations and NGOs:
Organizations like UNHCR, WHO, and various NGOs play a critical role in addressing HIV/AIDS in displacement settings. They can provide funding, technical support, and implement programs tailored to the needs of displaced populations.

Coordination and Collaboration:
Effective coordination between humanitarian organizations, host governments, and local communities is essential for the successful implementation of HIV/AIDS interventions.

HIV/AIDS presents significant challenges for displaced populations, but with coordinated efforts, these challenges can be addressed effectively. Prevention, treatment, and care must be integrated into the broader humanitarian response, with a focus on accessibility, inclusivity, and cultural sensitivity. By leveraging the strengths of international organizations, local communities, and healthcare systems, it is possible to mitigate the impact of HIV/AIDS among those in exile and improve their quality of life.

The explicatory of this chapter will offer a proper look at various scenarios that some haven't researched when needed – a world of information. Thus, they keep silent, letting other people express their views. Whatever doesn't meet people's expectations can be absolutely irritating, especially when others express it verbally, particularly political views.

Life has never seemed good to most of those in exile. Many times, when there's a change that motivates us, there's something to hinder what is about to occur in the lives of those patiently waiting to reap from the patience they have sewn.

One of the challenges we sometimes face is the indifference shown by autochthones. This is disturbing when we look at the same fellows, sharing the same oxygen, lands and all seasons in Africa. With such behaviour, we tend to be neurotic about the nasty statements made about us and denigrating names we have been branded with, showing those in exile that they don't count as human beings.

We have a real crisis which we wear like a garment when we're in certain situations such as the need to work in order to survive. However, we know that in South Africa, the first item requested is the green ID book which most people can't provide if they don't have permanent residence or citizenship. Thus, I find it so difficult being in South Africa and I believe it's a challenge which has affected thousands of immigrants.

It doesn't matter how you consider yourself or what consolation you offer to others. The truth is that you're undergoing a challenge which every individual experiences. It may not only apply to me, but there are many people who face challenges that I haven't experienced. In addition, I can speak on behalf of our brothers who constantly find it so challenging, on the verge of being dismissed, having been employed for some time, yet again becoming jobless. This is obviously disturbing psychologically.

Our *Creator's* purpose, according to the Bible, is for mankind to prosper in every area of life. He doesn't want us to continuously struggle. When we face challenges, we tend to compare our present struggle with past experiences to see if we can bring back any solutions we can apply now. Many people don't understand challenges and for others it has become a lifestyle. A lot of us don't care about the challenges these people face. This is because they have chosen to turn to drugs to forget their troubles. They forget they can't run away from the challenges which are there to strengthen us.

I've experienced a lot of challenges which seemed like a curse. I felt the need to ask my parents if they had placed one on me. Having asked them, I discovered it was merely my own thinking which had made me fear that.

In 2006, I began working as an alarm installer for *Pro Force Security*. It was a very important job because it was my living. After working there for a while, they discovered I was a foreigner. The discrimination I experienced was very similar to what I had faced in my previous job – having been born outside South Africa. When I realised the autochthones were treating me like an enemy, I decided to resign because of their allegations. I even feared people may poison me to get rid of me.

At this point, I didn't know what else to do. My studies at the varsity were on hold because I couldn't afford to pay my fees. I also had to pay rent which was a minimum of R2 800. A Zulu man had compassion on me as we discussed how to manage with what we had.

By God's grace, I came up with the idea to open my own business – an electronic repair shop. I thought at month end nobody would consider my need if I didn't do something for myself. Even though it was difficult at the beginning, I moved with perseverance until I stood with hope of victory. However, even if there was hope, I could undergo tough times, despite stressing every now and then. Life wasn't at all easy and, when I was in the house of the Lord, I felt peace. When the preacher spoke, he touched my heart, increasing my hope with his sermons. God's Word uplifted me.

Sometimes it's easy to say things off the cuff. However, when we experience something, we don't need to struggle to understand what it means when it occurs in an orderly fashion. During times of struggle, some have handled it well while others have blamed their backgrounds and the government. They have said it's because of selfishness and that may be the case. However, the only ones we believed deserved the blame were the politicians who presented a raw deal from the beginning, causing people to leave their beautiful homes.

In addition, they kept making empty promises to the nation. Thus, the women and children were the main victims. This became a national challenge. We wanted it a certain way but the politicians had their own ideas which had a negative effect on us. Thus, the purpose of these politicians was to manipulate people by challenging their self-esteem. When we say life hasn't been easy, we address the complaint regarding what had discouraged us. Most of those found in the same trap were puzzled about being victimised in the struggle.

Chapter 12

Challenge of power from the grave

The phenomenon of the "challenge of power from the grave" refers to a range of complex social, political, and psychological dynamics that arise when influential leaders or significant figures continue to exert control or inspire action even after their death. This influence can manifest through their ideas, legacies, institutional structures, written works, or fervent followers. Here are some ways this dynamic plays out and the implications it carries:

Political Influence

Posthumous Authority

Martyrdom:
Leaders who die under dramatic or tragic circumstances, especially if they are perceived as martyrs, can gain significant symbolic power. Their death can rally people to their cause and perpetuate their influence.

Symbolic Legacies:
The ideals and policies of deceased leaders are often enshrined in national consciousness, and subsequent leaders may invoke their names to garner support or legitimize their actions.

Institutional Structures

Enduring Policies:
Policies and institutions established by significant figures can outlive them, embedding their influence deeply into the fabric of society.

Dynastic Politics:
In some cases, family members or close associates may inherit the deceased leader's political mantle, continuing their legacy and influence.

Cultural and Social Impact

Cultural Icons

Eternal Fame:
Cultural figures such as artists, thinkers, and activists often achieve a form of immortality through their work, continuing to inspire and shape societal values long after their death.

Cultural Narratives:
Stories and myths surrounding a figure's life and deeds can become deeply embedded in cultural narratives, influencing future generations.

Memorialization

Monuments and Memorials:
Erecting monuments, memorials, and holidays in honor of deceased figures serves to reinforce their memory and propagate their values.

Educational Curricula:
The inclusion of their life and work in educational curricula ensures their continued relevance and influence on young minds.

Religious and Spiritual Influence

Canonization and Sainthood

Saints and Prophets:
In many religious traditions, deceased figures who demonstrated exceptional virtues, piety, or prophetic vision are canonized or revered as saints, continuing to guide the spiritual lives of followers.

Religious Texts:
Sacred texts attributed to or associated with these figures often become central to the faith and are studied, interpreted, and followed by adherents.

Cult of Personality

Idolization:
In extreme cases, the personality cults that develop around influential figures can transform them into quasi-divine beings, with followers attributing supernatural qualities to them even after death.

Psychological and Emotional Impact

Trauma of Loss

Grief and Mourning:
The death of a highly influential or beloved figure can cause widespread grief and mourning, impacting collective psychology and social behavior.

Legacy Pressure:
Individuals or communities closely associated with the deceased may feel intense pressure to uphold or live up to their perceived legacy.

Negative Legacies

Oppressive Regimes

Authoritarian Residue:
The influence of authoritarian leaders can persist through

the structures they established, such as surveillance apparatus, legal frameworks, or cultural norms, continuing to oppress and control populations.

Ghost of Ideologies:
Harmful ideologies propagated by deceased figures can survive through followers or institutional inertia, continuing to cause societal harm or conflict.

Historical Revisionism

Manipulation of Legacy:
The legacies of controversial figures may be manipulated or revised by various interest groups, either to discredit or glorify them, affecting public perception and historical discourse.

Addressing the Challenge

Critical Engagement

Historical Analysis:
It's crucial to engage critically with the legacies of influential figures, recognizing both their contributions and their flaws. This balanced understanding can prevent blind veneration or vilification.

Public Discourse:
Open public discourse about the merits and drawbacks of a figure's legacy can foster a healthier societal relationship with their memory.

Cultural Literacy

Education:
Promoting cultural and historical literacy helps individuals contextualize the lives and works of past figures, understanding the complexities of their influence.

Commemoration Practices:
Rethinking how societies commemorate influential figures,

embracing inclusive and multi-faceted approaches to remembrance that reflect diverse perspectives.

The "challenge of power from the grave" is a testament to the enduring impact that influential figures can have on society, both positively and negatively. It highlights the importance of critically engaging with historical legacies, fostering public discourse, and promoting cultural literacy to ensure that the influence of past figures continues to benefit society while mitigating potential harms. Through these efforts, societies can navigate the complex interplay of memory, legacy, and power in a nuanced and constructive

This one cannot be seen as superstition. Thus, it is another invisible force that couldn't appear to anyone else but was felt by those who were in its presence. I regretted losing my girlfriend – the mother of my daughter, Thabit Dorcas. It was a while back when my daughter and I lost her mother who was very dear to us. Her death greatly confused me. I was unable to trace the truth about our relationship and that was dreadful.

If you read the first few chapters, you will have a clear understanding concerning the whole story I've written concerning my girlfriend and daughter. I first denied my daughter because of the foundation her mother had laid, based on lies which were exposed after some time. Infidelity is evil because, when someone is unfaithful, they may experience pleasure, but when it's exposed, it brings a sense of condemnation, making the perpetrator wonder why he or she succumbed to temptation.

When I was convinced the baby was mine, the girl left me. It took more than five years to accept that I could still function as a normal man after admitting she was my baby. It may seem that I accepted the baby because I was afraid of the mother's reaction, but that really wasn't the case. The only reason I went back was to connect with the baby I believed was mine.

One Sunday when I was having a nap, I felt something strange I hadn't felt before. At around 14H15, whilst in bed, it felt as if a strong fever had gripped me. I tried unsuccessfully to reach for my pyjamas even though they were near me. I tried to call someone in a room near mine but my mouth wouldn't open though my eyes were. I was unaware that one of my tenants was facing a horrific moment by what seemed to be the ghost of my late girlfriend appearing to her while she was asleep. The girl struggled to scream while she was being strangled by the ghost. The moment she was able to escape, she rushed into my bedroom. I asked her what that was. She told me a strange story which she had from reading the ghost's lips about a baby and she kept repeating the same thing. I decided to call my late girlfriend's aunt so I could explain to her what had taken place. It was an experience that shook me.

We need to face a challenge with confidence. This is a bit tricky as we know they can be tough and people can act strangely just because they're trying to cover that up. Sometimes, we do feel the punch of a challenge and complain. But the pain won't be the same when we're faced with a global economic crisis.

We may have cried, but we didn't demonstrate how much it had affected us. The truth is, I didn't know how severe things were for them. However, my complaint was so amplified because I'd felt it in all areas. I kept quiet after considering its level and the speed with which it came.

At that time, South Africans were presented with high bills which affected everyone. I personally was paying approximately R200 per month as far as my consumption was concerned. There came a time when electricity bills increased to R1 800 and I wasn't the only one affected. Many people complained about this issue which was a big challenge to every person who lived in Durban Central.

If this crisis shook citizens then, how much more now will

it be for those helpless with no vacancies or connections whatsoever? These were issues to look at very carefully and realise the severity thereof.

Challenge! It's all about challenge!. In this case, it cannot be seen only from an African perspective but also in European countries and others such as Asia. I believe the spirit powers from the grave are demons from the Christian perspective. Most of those who believe in Christianity do not entertain whoever appears to them as one of their brothers, sisters, uncles, aunts or anyone who played a relative role in the family. There is always the eradication of such a spirit. It doesn't matter how dearly that particular person was in the lives of those who were left.

In this chapter, it may not seem relevant to you but I wrote it with knowledge that was supported by the experience I had during the past few years. To other people, what I call 'power from the grave' is the appearance of a 'dead person' and is viewed as a visitor from the grave. Others view it as personal visitation and they even build a room or something to honour that ghost. However, I think my experiences were enough for me to understand that this cannot be entertained because it is a spirit.

Some African countries, due to culture, acknowledge this as part of their worship. Most in these categories embrace it as giving them solutions to their problems. However, we must understand there is no way back when somebody is dead to return to earth. It is absolutely false.

Christians believe they will go to Heaven. My point is metaphorically given and, if you look at it, you'll recognise that, whatever may appear to you, if you think it's a particular person after death, a question arises:

- *Is there an exit in Heaven?*
- *Is there a way out of Hell?*
- *When our loved ones eventually die, will they go either*

to Heaven or Hell.

- *If they were able to return to this life on earth, that would mean there is a way out of either Heaven or Hell.*

This theory would make God a liar

The reason why I call them ghosts is because they are spirits. They show up in the form and appearance of our loved ones. When they appear, they come with strange forces that seem to be irresistible to those who are alive. There is always a change in atmosphere and the temperature can rise to a great heat.

Chapter 13

Justice and injustice in exile

The concepts of justice and injustice in exile encompass a range of issues related to the fair and equitable treatment – or lack thereof – of refugees, internally displaced persons (IDPs), asylum seekers, and other individuals living in displacement. The justice system's ability to protect these individuals' rights or, conversely, the failure to do so, has far-reaching implications for their well-being, dignity, and future prospects. Here's an in-depth examination of these concepts in the context of exile:

Justice in Exile

Legal Protections and Rights

International Legal Frameworks

Refugee Convention (1951):
This key document sets out the rights of refugees and the obligations of states to protect them. It includes principles like non-refoulement (not returning refugees to a place where they face serious threat) and access to basic rights (e.g., education, work).

International Human Rights Law:
Instruments such as the Universal Declaration of

Human Rights (UDHR) provide broader protections that apply to all individuals, including those in exile.

Access to Asylum

Fair Process:
Ensuring access to a fair and efficient asylum process is crucial. This includes due process rights, the right to appeal decisions, and freedom from arbitrary detention.

Legal Aid and Representation

Access to Legal Counsel:
Providing refugees and asylum seekers with access to legal representation can help them navigate complex legal systems and better defend their rights in asylum proceedings.

Social Justice

Access to Services:
Healthcare, Education, and Housing: Ensuring displaced persons have access to essential services is a matter of social justice. This includes both emergency aid and long-term support.

Employment Rights

Right to Work:
Allowing refugees and displaced persons to work legally can help them achieve self-reliance and dignity, reducing dependency on aid and promoting integration.

Community Support

Integration and Inclusion:
Encouraging host communities to integrate displaced persons through programs that promote mutual

understanding and respect can foster social cohesion and justice.

Protection from Violence and Exploitation

Safety from Conflict and Persecution

Host Country Obligations:
Host countries must ensure the physical safety and security of displaced individuals, protecting them from violence, exploitation, and human trafficking.

Gender-Based Protections

Specific Vulnerabilities:
Addressing the specific needs of women, children, and LGBTQ+ individuals who may face heightened risks of violence and exploitation is essential for achieving justice in exile.

Injustice in Exile

Legal Injustices

Arbitrary Detention:
Detention Conditions: Prolonged or arbitrary detention of refugees and asylum seekers, often in inhumane conditions, represents a significant injustice and a violation of international law.

Barriers to Asylum

Restricted Access:
Policies that bar or severely restrict access to asylum, such as pushbacks at borders or externalization agreements, prevent individuals from exercising their right to seek protection.

Lack of Legal Protection:

Statelessness: The lack of legal identity or recognition (e.g., statelessness) leaves many people in exile without basic legal protections, making them vulnerable to rights violations.

Social Injustices

Discrimination and Xenophobia

Hostility in Host Countries:
Refugees and displaced persons often face discrimination, xenophobia, and social exclusion in host countries, affecting their ability to integrate and access services.

Inadequate Living Conditions

Substandard Camps and Shelters:
Many displaced persons live in overcrowded and unsanitary conditions, lacking access to basic amenities and services.

Economic Exploitation

Illegal Employment:
The lack of legal work opportunities can push displaced persons into exploitative labor situations, where they are subject to low wages, poor working conditions, and abuse.

Protection Gaps

Gender-Based Violence

Insufficient Response:
The failure to adequately prevent and respond to gender-based violence, including sexual exploitation and abuse, is a major injustice faced by many women and girls in exile.

Child Protection Failures

Unaccompanied Minors:
Children, particularly unaccompanied minors, are at significant risk of trafficking, exploitation, and abuse, with inadequate systems in place to protect them.

Mental Health Neglect

Psychological Impact:
The traumatic experiences of displacement, coupled with ongoing stress and uncertainty, can lead to

- *Does the South African Government apply justice to foreigners?*
- *Do we have access to the justice we deserve?*
- *Are we satisfied with the rights we think we have?*
- *Is there anything we believe is beyond our reach?*
- *How do we know what justice and injustice are?*
- *What do we want in all this?*

These are questions I faced during the time I started observing the system that South Africa had toward foreigners. Those who experienced justice happened to be knowledgeable which gave them the confidence to know their rights.

With these posed questions, my concerns accumulated which I had spent at least two to four hours trying to work on. When will this tribulation end? We are living in this reality but they want us to hide it in order to entertain their self-esteem. We cannot afford to cater to their esteem whereby we ourselves are in conflict with the government when we were only offered this opportunity to be in South Africa conditionally. If we can't learn something from them, they are useless in our country.

For a long time, some people didn't know they're not here in vain as they are sustained by the UNHCR. This is mostly for refugees and for those in South Africa by visa who also have the right to obtain whatever they need. However, some people don't know they have rights, especially when they realise there is an agreement established between the Government and the UNHCR. That's when the people began to stand up for their rights.

Chapter 14

Justice, love and truth

The interplay of justice, love, and truth in the context of exile the profound human dimensions involved in the experiences of displaced persons. These elements are crucial for restoring dignity, fostering resilience, and promoting healing for individuals and communities affected by displacement. Here's an exploration of how justice, love, and truth manifest and interact within the circumstances of exile:

Justice in Exile

Legal and Human Rights Protections

Fair Legal Processes:
Asylum and Refugee Status Determination: Establishing fair, transparent, and efficient legal processes for determining refugee status and granting asylum is essential to uphold the rights of displaced individuals.

Due Process:
Providing procedural safeguards, including the right to appeal decisions and access to legal representation, ensures that individuals have a fair chance to make their case.

Access to Basic Rights:
Education, Health Care, and Housing: Ensuring access to essential services is a matter of justice. Displaced

persons must be able to secure the necessities of life to live with dignity.

Employment Rights:
Legal permission to work empowers displaced individuals economically, reduces dependency on aid, and facilitates social integration.

Protection from Harm

Physical Safety:
Host countries must protect refugees and displaced persons from violence, exploitation, and abuse, including gender-based violence and child exploitation.

Legal Status:
Providing legal recognition and documentation can prevent statelessness and ensure that displaced persons have access to their rights.

**Love in Exile –
Human Compassion and Solidarity**

Welcoming Attitudes

Community Support:
Host communities that embrace displaced persons with compassion and empathy foster an environment where individuals feel valued and respected.

Volunteer and NGO work:
Many local and international volunteers and organizations provide essential services and support, acting out of a sense of love and solidarity.

Emotional and Psychological Support

Mental Health Services:
Providing mental health care and counseling helps

displaced individuals cope with trauma, loss, and the challenges of displacement.

Social Connections:
Encouraging social interaction and building community networks can help displaced persons form new social bonds and reduce isolation.

Restoring Dignity

Empowerment:
Initiatives that empower displaced persons to have agency over their lives – including educational programs, vocational training, and leadership opportunities – promote a sense of dignity and self-worth.

Cultural Preservation:
Maintaining cultural traditions and practices in exile can help individuals retain a sense of identity and continuity amidst the upheaval.

Truth in Exile – Acknowledgement and Transparency

Acknowledging Experiences

Truth-Telling:
Recognizing and documenting the stories and experiences of displaced persons is crucial. This includes understanding the causes of their displacement and the injustices they have faced.

Historical Records:
Creating historical records and archives that capture the experiences of exile can ensure that these narratives are preserved and acknowledged.

Combating Misconceptions

Public Education:

Educating the public about the realities of displacement, the contributions of displaced persons, and the challenges they face can counteract stigma, misinformation, and xenophobia.

Media Representation:
Accurate and empathetic representation of displaced persons in the media reflects their true experiences and counters harmful stereotypes.

Justice Mechanisms

Accountability:
Holding perpetrators of violence and injustice accountable through legal and international mechanisms reinforces the principle of truth in addressing past wrongs.

Restorative Justice:
Approaches that focus on healing and reconciliation, rather than solely on punishment, can help address the wounds caused by injustice and displacement.

Between Justice, Love, and Truth

Building a Just and Compassionate Society

Holistic Support Systems

Integrated Approaches:
Combining legal advocacy, humanitarian assistance, and psychosocial support creates comprehensive systems that address the multifaceted needs of displaced persons.

Policy and Practice:
Policies informed by justice, love, and truth ensure that responses to displacement are humane, effective, and sustainable.

Community Engagement

Inclusive Policymaking:
Involving displaced persons in policymaking processes ensures that their voices are heard and that policies reflect their real needs and aspirations.

Grassroots Initiatives:
Community-led initiatives often embody the principles of justice, love, and truth, as they are rooted in the lived experiences and strengths of displaced communities.

Global Solidarity

nternational Cooperation:
Global solidarity and cooperation, guided by the principles of justice, love, and truth, are essential to address the root causes of displacement

Socrates, an ancient Greek philosopher, came up with the same formula to make people think by asking what love, truth and justice are. We cannot embrace justice without love and, in order to demonstrate love, we need to have truth within us because there is no justice without love and truth. When we lack truth, justice cannot exist. We need love and truth to give justice its meaning. If we look at how things are done in a court of law, we'll find justice's dwelling place.

Sometimes we view justice in its correct context but those we thought would demonstrate it are the ones who defile it. *So where is justice?* In police stations, there are strong rules and regulations, yet the same police officers are the ones who break them.

The law stipulates that we must respect the rules and conditions on the roads but the question is do they respect it? To jump a robot is a very big infraction to us. Is it also the same to them? We are told not to drink and drive which is very important. The question is, do the authorities set the example? Many times we are warned to not take the law into our own hands but the truth is that the same people who prohibit these acts are the first to disobey them.

It was hard for me to be accused and apprehended for something I hadn't done. However, whilst I was in custody, my eyes were opened because I wanted to know whether justice worked in South Africa. However, I knew that justice works – according to the appointed judge. Before I experienced justice, the first thing I encountered was injustice displayed by the autochthones.

If justice isn't mixed with atrocities, it's one of the strongest channels that keeps the country leading a proper legislation. If justice isn't operative in the country, it then leads to abuse of authority which creates a downfall. Justice must be served fairly and righteously. Many times, the innocent are victimised and judged. Their punishment appears to be more than those who were actually guilty of particular atrocities.

When we're told we have the right to remain silent, that is actually what they want – everyone to obey what they preach, yet don't practise. They use the word 'justice' as a password to cruelty and, in addition to this, some don't really know what to do. When we follow their instructions politely, the only thing we find is the disregard of ordinary people. Then, when someone calls for help, no-one comes to his or her rescue.

When I called for help, I expected to receive justice wherein I would be defended in order to have peace of heart and mind. All I experienced was people who had no compassion on me.

Chapter 15

The nature of justice

The nature of justice is a deeply complex and multifaceted concept that has occupied philosophers, legal scholars, theologians, and sociologists for millennia. It touches upon principles of fairness, equity, morality, and the proper ordering of society. Here we delve into the various dimensions and theories that shape our understanding of justice:

Philosophical Foundations

Classical Theories

Plato (Ideal Justice):
In his work *"The Republic,"* Plato sees justice as a virtue that exists when each part of society and each part of the soul performs its appropriate function. For Plato, justice is tied to the idea of the Good and is achieved through harmony and balance.

Aristotle (Distributive and Corrective Justice):
Aristotle distinguishes between distributive justice (the fair allocation of resources in proportion to individuals' merits) and corrective justice (restoring balance when harm has been done). He emphasizes the importance of equality and the role of law in achieving justice.

Modern Theories

John Rawls (Theory of Justice as Fairness)

Rawls proposes two principles of justice:
(1) The principle of equal basic liberties, and (2) The difference principle, which allows social and economic inequalities only if they benefit the least advantaged members of society. He uses the hypothetical 'original position' and 'veil of ignorance' to argue for fairness in decision-making.

Robert Nozick (Libertarian Justice):
Nozick challenges Rawls with his entitlement theory, which focuses on justice in acquisition, transfer, and rectification of holdings. He argues that a just distribution of resources results from fair processes, not necessarily equal outcomes.

Legal and Political Dimensions

Rule of Law and Legal Systems

Impartiality and Equality Before the Law:
One key aspect of justice is the idea that laws should be applied impartially and equally, without favoritism or bias. This is fundamental to the rule of law.

Human Rights and Civil Liberties:
Ensuring that all individuals have access to fundamental human rights and freedoms, such as freedom of speech, equality before the law, and protection from arbitrary detention, is central to legal justice.

Social Justice

Economic and Social Equity:
Social justice concerns itself with the distribution of wealth, opportunities, and privileges within a society.

It seeks to address inequalities and ensure that all individuals have access to basic needs and opportunities for advancement.

Institutional Fairness:
Institutions, including the judicial system, educational system, and healthcare system, must operate fairly and serve all members of society adequately.

Moral and Ethical Perspectives

Utilitarianism

Greatest Happiness Principle:
Utilitarian theories of justice, such as those proposed by Jeremy Bentham and John Stuart Mill, argue that justice is achieved when actions promote the greatest happiness for the greatest number. Policies and laws should be judged by their consequences in terms of overall well-being.

Deontological Ethics

Duty and Rights-Based Justice:
Immanuel Kant's ethical theory focuses on duty and adherence to moral rules or principles. Justice, in this view, involves respecting the rights and dignity of all individuals, regardless of the outcomes.

Restorative and Retributive Justice

Retributive Justice

Punishment and Deterrence:
 Retributive justice is based on the idea that wrongdoers deserve to be punished proportionately to their offenses. This form of justice serves to deter future wrongdoing and affirm societal norms.

Restorative Justice

Reconciliation and Repair:
Restorative justice focuses on repairing the harm caused by criminal behavior. It emphasizes reconciliation between the offender and the victim and involves community participation in the justice process. The aim is healing, rather than punishment.

Contemporary Issues and Challenges

Global Justice

nternational Law and Human Rights:
The nature of justice extends beyond national borders, encompassing issues of global justice such as international human rights, global inequality, and responses to crises like climate change and refugee movements.

Cultural Relativism:
Justice may be viewed differently across various cultures. Understanding and respecting these differences while finding common ground is a significant contemporary challenge.

Intersectionality

Multiple Dimensions of Inequality:
Justice must consider how various forms of inequality intersect, such as race, gender, class, and sexuality. An intersectional approach seeks to address the compounded injustices faced by individuals at these intersections.

Spiritual and Religious Dimensions

Spiritual Concepts of Justice:
Many religious traditions carry their unique

interpretations of justice. For instance, in Christianity, justice is often linked with the notion of divine righteousness and mercy. In Islam, justice (Adl) is a fundamental concept that involves fairness and fulfilling obligations.

Having titled this chapter *The nature of justice,* I would like to demonstrate a very crucial issue. For example, should we be leading a particular group, we should first have enthusiasm to perform in accordance with what draws people's interest. The project must be fair, promoting justice.

When we downgrade justice, we play a cruel game which subverts the whole system from where truth originates. However, in South Africa, justice is polluted because, when we carefully follow how justice is offered, we find everything is determined by choice and selection. We can choose something but, when we do, we become responsible for it.

Regarding choice, there's a certain intensity which influences the ability thereof from where it was derived. That's why, when deciding what to choose, there are aspects presented which, motivated by our desire for justice, brings freedom in many spheres of life.

Due to the lack of justice, if we don't have any means to defend our innocence, we will suffer. We must know that justice costs money in South Africa. This shouldn't be the case. *True justice* must be offered freely and fairly without having to pay for it.

Every person has the right to live according to his optimum. Only now are we discovering how to express our feelings toward these issues.

Chapter **16**

Injustice involved

Exile, the forced removal or displacement of individuals or communities from their homelands, often brings about a myriad of injustices. These injustices can be multifaceted, impacting various aspects of life, and can extend over long periods of time. Here's an in-depth exploration of the different types of injustices involved in exile:

Legal and Political Injustice

Denial of Legal Rights and Protections

Statelessness:
Exiled individuals may become stateless, losing their nationality and the legal protections that come with it. This can leave them vulnerable to exploitation and without access to rights such as employment, education, and healthcare.

Arbitrary Detention:
Exiled individuals, especially refugees, can face arbitrary detention in host countries, often without due process or legal recourse.

Political Exploitation and Persecution

Persecution:
Exiles are frequently the result of political persecution, where individuals are targeted due to their beliefs, ethnicity, religion, or political activities.

Lack of Representation:
Exiled individuals often lack political representation in their home and host countries, leaving them without a voice in matters that affect their lives.

Economic Injustice

Loss of Livelihood and Economic Opportunity

Employment Barriers:
Exiled individuals frequently face significant barriers to employment in host countries, including legal restrictions, discrimination, and credential recognition issues.

Poverty and Dependency:
The inability to secure stable and sufficient employment often leads to poverty and dependence on humanitarian aid, which can be unreliable and inadequate.

Resource Denial

Asset Confiscation:
Exile often involves the loss of personal and communal assets, such as homes, land, and businesses, which may be confiscated or rendered inaccessible.

Loss of Social Capital:
Exiled individuals lose the social networks and community ties that are often crucial for economic opportunities and support.

Social and Cultural Injustice

Cultural Displacement and Identity Erosion

Cultural Erasure:
Exiled communities may face pressures to assimilate into host cultures, which can lead to the erosion of their cultural practices, languages, and traditions.

Identity Crisis:
The forced separation from homeland and community can trigger identity crises, as individuals struggle to maintain their cultural identity in a foreign environment.

Social Isolation and Discrimination

Marginalization:
Exiled individuals often experience social marginalization and isolation in host countries, exacerbated by language barriers, social stigma, and xenophobia.

Discrimination and Racism:
Prejudice and discrimination in host countries can permeate various aspects of life, from housing and employment to education and healthcare.

Emotional and Psychological Injustice

Trauma and Mental Health

Psychological Trauma:
The experience of exile is often traumatic, involving violence, loss, and severe upheaval. This trauma can lead to long-term mental health issues such as depression, anxiety, and PTSD.

Lack of Mental Health Services:
Access to appropriate mental health services is often limited for exiled individuals, either due to lack of resources or cultural and linguistic barriers.

Family Separation and Breakdown

Separation from Family:
Exile frequently results in the separation of families, with members scattered across different countries or regions, leading to emotional distress and weakening of familial support systems.

Disruption of Social Structures:
The breakdown of larger community and kinship networks disrupts traditional social structures and support systems that are vital for emotional well-being.

Educational Injustice

Barrier to Education

Access to Education:
Exiled individuals, particularly children, often face barriers to accessing education, including legal restrictions, language barriers, and lack of infrastructure.

Quality of Education:
When education is accessible, it is often of lower quality, provided in overcrowded, under-resourced settings, and may not be recognized by host or home countries.

Interruption in Learning and Development

Disrupted Education:
The abrupt disruption of education due to exile can have long-term impacts on individuals' learning and development, limiting future opportunities and contributing to a cycle of poverty.

Health Injustice

Access to Healthcare

Healthcare Barriers:
Exiled populations often face significant barriers to accessing healthcare, including legal restrictions, lack of insurance, and language and cultural barriers.

Substandard Living Conditions:
Poor living conditions in exile, such as overcrowded refugee camps or inadequate housing, heighten health risks and exacerbate existing health conditions.

Public Health Risks

Disease and Malnutrition:
Exiled individuals are at increased risk of infectious diseases, malnutrition, and other health crises due to limited access to clean

When injustice is involved, we ask questions such as: *"Why do they act like this?" "How can they do this to me?"* We declare our innocence. When we're victimised and falsely accused, it's necessary to find the real perpetrator.

There was a time when I was confronted by a South African policeman. This scenario took place in the shop where I was working as a technician in electronics. He began to speak to me regarding hatred and jealousy. His approach was provocative. I didn't respond in an aggressive manner. After having been interrogated, I attentively followed him.

He then handed me an iron, requesting me to repair it. I examined it in his presence and told him how much it would cost. I repaired it. Five weeks later, he returned, complaining that the iron had the same problem again.

This was absolutely false as, at first, the iron didn't function at all. I discovered a broken element containing water. Switching it on would trip the power in the house. He left, disappearing for about 20 weeks. He finally returned with the intention of seizing my work tools. I refused to give them to him. This resulted in a physical combat. We were both wounded. I began to slow down and trid to calm him. I managed to escape and headed for the police station. He chased me, viciously punching me at the robot. I then became very angry and retaliated. However, spectators could see I had been trying to avoid him. They could tell from his violent behaviour that I was his target. At that point, both of us were put in jail. Where was the justice?

His attack on me was a great injustice. The policeman's colleagues didn't want to know who had started it. They victimised me, accusing me of being the troublemaker. I was supposed to open a case against him but he implored me to forget the incident, pretending to make peace with me as he knew he was due to be in training in Pretoria.

We forgave each other and were released. Four weeks later, he opened a case against me whilst away from the province. He instructed police to apprehend me. I went to prison without having any idea why I had been arrested. I was later told it was the policeman who had publicly assaulted me. I found it very unfair and inconsiderate that he had opened a case against me when I had forgiven him.

This was another side of injustice to me. I spent approximately a year appearing in court without seeing the policeman who opened the case against me. When the man failed to attend, the case was withdrawn. However, the injustice was evident as I had to appear many times alone in the courtroom.

Chapter **17**

A time to embrace justice

Embracing justice is an imperative that calls for concerted efforts across, societal, institutional, and global levels to ensure fairness, equity, and respect for human dignity. Here are some actionable steps for embracing justice:

Personal Level

Self-Education and Awareness

Educate Yourself:
Learn about different forms of injustice, including social, economic, racial, and environmental injustices. Understand their historical contexts and current manifestations.

Reflect on Biases:
Examine your own biases and prejudices. Develop a habit of self-reflection to recognize and address unconscious biases.

Advocacy and Activism

Speak Out:
Use your voice to advocate for justice. Speak out against injustices in your community, workplace, or social circles.

Volunteer:
Support organizations that work towards justice, whether through volunteering your time, skills, or resources.

Community Level

Promoting Inclusivity and Equity

Foster Inclusive Communities:
Create and support environments that are inclusive and equitable. This can include promoting diversity in local clubs, schools, workplaces, and other community spaces.

Support Marginalized Groups:
Advocate for and support marginalized and underrepresented groups within your community.

Community Engagement

Participate in Civic Activities:
Engage in local governance processes. Attend town hall meetings, vote in local elections, and encourage others to become active participants in civic life.

Restorative Practices:
Encourage the use of restorative practices to address conflicts and harm within the community, focusing on reconciliation and healing rather than punishment.

Institutional Level

Policy and Legal Reform

Advocate for Fair Policies:
Support policies and legislation that promote justice and tackle systemic inequalities. Pressure policymakers to implement and enforce laws that protect human rights and promote fairness.

Legal Aid and Services:
Support legal aid services that provide assistance to those who cannot afford it, ensuring access to justice for all.

Institutional Accountability

Transparency and Accountability:
Promote transparency and accountability within institutions, including governments, corporations, and law enforcement agencies. Hold these entities accountable for unjust practices.

Inclusive Representation:
Advocate for diverse and inclusive representation within institutional decision-making bodies to ensure that all voices are heard and considered.

Global Level

Human Rights Advocacy

Support International Justice Mechanisms:
Support international organizations and mechanisms that work to uphold human rights and deliver justice on a global scale, such as the International Criminal Court (ICC) and United Nations agencies.

Global Solidarity:
Engage in global solidarity movements that aim to address global injustices, such as climate change, poverty, and displacement. Support initiatives that promote global equity and sustainable development.

Addressing Global Inequities

Fair Trade:
Promote and support fair trade practices that ensure equitable treatment and compensation for producers in developing countries.

Humanitarian Assistance:
Support humanitarian organizations that provide aid and support to those affected by crises, focusing on long-term development and resilience-building in addition to immediate relief.

Educational Initiatives

Teaching and Learning for Justice

Education for Justice:
Incorporate social justice education in curricula at all levels. Teach students about the importance of justice, human rights, and ethical responsibility.

Lifelong Learning:
Promote lifelong learning opportunities focused on justice, including community workshops, public lectures, and online courses.

Critical Thinking and Empathy

Develop Critical Thinking:
Encourage critical thinking skills to challenge unjust narratives, question status quos, and seek evidence-based solutions.

Foster Empathy:
Promote empathy and understanding through storytelling, cultural exchange programs, and dialogue initiatives that bring different communities together.

Corporate Responsibility

Ethical Business Practices

Corporate Social Responsibility (CSR):

Encourage businesses to adopt ethical practices and CSR initiatives that promote justice, such as fair labor practices, sustainability efforts, and community engagement.

Diversity and Inclusion:
Advocate for diversity and inclusion within corporate structures, ensuring that all employees have the opportunity to succeed and thrive.

Equitable Economic Practices

Living Wages:
Support and implement policies that ensure living wages and fair compensation for all workers.

Consumer Advocacy:
As consumers, support companies with ethical practices and hold accountable those that engage in exploitative or unjust behaviors.

Embracing justice is a continuous, multifaceted effort that requires engagement at every level of society. It demands a commitment to fairness, equality, and respect for human dignity. By adopting these actionable steps, individuals and communities can work towards creating a more just and equitable world for all. The collective endeavor to embrace justice is not only a moral imperative but also a path to fostering a more harmonious,

The time for prevarication has gone. Now is the time to tell what we are daily facing, caused by the giants of this world who refuse to show up with a sense of humour. They prefer to subvert according to their nature. They share our oxygen, shop in the same shops, pretending to share the same religions and filled with sweet talk. However, the moment they're on their thrones, they have no time to discern what truth is all about. They hurt innocent people around them. How long must we keep undergoing such torment? Should we continue in this situation? What will our children's future be then? In this case, it seems we may be enslaved again because, during slavery, the oppressors used injustice as the keyword for choice which affected the systems of rulership in so many sectors due to leadership.

If we talk about systems regarding choice in South Africa, there's so much injustice. Political inability shows in the facet whereby South African criteria in the police force has caused too much damage on recruiting people unfit to be in the force. The song they sing is injustice, corruption and discrimination, resulting in foreigners in South Africa having troubled minds even though they believe it's their land as Africans.

This should be a time to embrace justice, not injustice, in order to return to the natural foundation which is to put on a sense of humour, leading to natural priorities where we shall find all principles of laws attached to any human sentiment.

I've interviewed different people concerning justice and injustice and, during interviews, I've learned that everyone has different opinions, cementing the same reality. Most of the people were males but, at this point, I spoke to a Zimbabwean woman in order to bring light from a female's perspective on justice. She responded negatively, stating that injustice exists in South Africa.

Our fellow brothers have displayed discrimination which is a strong weapon, placing a lot of pressure on foreigners. They don't consider Africans who come from other parts of Africa. They don't treat them valuably but regard them like animals, forgetting they are also Africans like others.

In the same manner, we've lost a lot of people. Some were beaten to death; others were gunned down and the remnant are living in the fear that anything can happen at any time. This places a sense of hopelessness in people. If we remain victimised, we cannot sing the song of justice because we have been told we don't belong in South Africa. For those who have been granted permanent residences in this country hoping to be established, they are as they were in days gone by.

To be more explicit, this is a very intense issue. There are questions that sometimes rise up concerning ownership, some of them being:

- *"How do you feel when facing rejection in your own land, being fully aware of your identity?"*
- *"How do you feel when you're told you don't belong, being regarded as a total stranger in your own land?"*
- *"If an African man doesn't belong in Africa, where then does he belong?"*

Regarding injustice in South Africa, many immigrants have suffered from the very same thing by local people, causing them to turn to evil ways just to protect themselves. My views are indeed clear toward these issues, especially regarding the police force. There has been a deep injustice done underhandedly to immigrants. Many have been affected but there's nothing they can do about it. Whoever attempts to speak up faces a verbal insult which will either denigrate him or he's told to go and complain in his own country. Many local people have lost a sense of humanity, not because that's the way the Creator of Heaven and Earth designed it, but it's the way South African men have made it. This issue seems to be ongoing.

Many times, we foreigners face injustice directly due to xenophobia. Male autochthones are even more vicious than females. This kind of behaviour toward other humanitarians accelerates in most sectors in South Africa. So where is the justice?

I remember the time I worked in electronics. I had a specialty with appliances. A police officer violently invaded my private workspace and we were both detained even though I was the one who had been attacked by the officer. Later on, the law officers turned against me. My explanation to the other police officers was ignored because I couldn't speak their language. Therefore, my views on justice were constrained due to the suspension I was given.

- The police officer received a lump sum of money. The investigation made by the detectives as well as the magistrate and the prosecutor favoured the police officer whereby their final assessment also took place indicating that the police officer was right in everything.

I then realised injustice has a foundation which will take at least three decades to be uprooted, requiring a combination of nations. Otherwise, South Africa will lose its dignity. *Other than that, things will remain as they are.*

Conclusion

Living in exile is undoubtedly a challenging experience, fraught with uncertainties, dislocation, and the pain of leaving behind one's homeland. Yet, through resilience, adaptability, and the pursuit of stability, social connections, personal growth, and cultural preservation, it is possible to find fulfillment and meaning in this journey.

Key Takeaways for a Fulfilled Life in Exile:

Establish Stability and Security:
- Secure legal and financial stability to build a solid foundation in your new environment.
- Ensure safe and comfortable housing to foster a sense of security.

Build a Support Network:
- Engage with community groups and build supportive relationships to combat isolation and foster belonging.
- Seek to reunite with family members whenever possible, leveraging familial support and unity.

Focus on Well-being:
- Prioritize mental, emotional, and physical health through counseling, self-care, and maintaining a healthy lifestyle.
- Regularly access healthcare services and engage in activities that promote overall well-being.

Pursue Education and Skill Development:
- Learn the local language and continue your education to enhance integration and increase opportunities.
- Develop new skills through vocational training and

further education, enabling better prospects for employment.

Seek Employment and Economic Empowerment:
- Utilize job search assistance programs and network actively to find employment opportunities.
- Consider entrepreneurship and explore funding opportunities to achieve financial independence and personal fulfillment.

Maintain Cultural Identity:
- Preserve and celebrate cultural traditions, ensuring a sense of continuity and identity.
- Share your culture with locals to foster mutual respect and understanding, and join cultural organizations to stay connected with your heritage.

Set and Pursue Goals:
- Define realistic short-term and long-term goals to stay focused and motivated.
- Celebrate milestones and achievements to maintain morale and a sense of progress.

Navigating life in exile is a profound journey that demands courage, flexibility, and hope. While the path is often strewn with obstacles, it is also paved with opportunities for growth, connection, and fulfillment. By actively seeking stability, building a supportive network, prioritizing well-being, continuing education, seeking economic empowerment, maintaining cultural identity, and setting personal goals, individuals in exile can rebuild their lives and find meaning in their new circumstances.

Ultimately, the experience of exile can foster resilience, deepen empathy, and broaden perspectives, enriching not only the lives of those who traverse it but also the communities that welcome them. Through steadfast determination and collective support, a fulfilling and purposeful life in exile is achievable, paving the way for a brighter future and a renewed sense of belonging.

ಬಾಃಬ

This is my story related to the hardship encountered way back after my wrongful arrest by a police officer. Later, after being trapped by the law, I was found in the position whereby my explanation seemed meaningless.

Though the law turned against me, I was very disappointed and at the same time, hurt. This incident made me feel as if the law favours certain people and others become victims of that particular favouritism. The first unjustified thing that transpired was that, when I couldn't speak the vernacular language, my rights were denied immediately. Therefore, I realized that injustice has profoundly been rooted in almost every sector. Africans have become enemies among themselves.

Another thing that predominately transpires in South Africa, which caused havoc from time to time between the citizens and other brothers coming from around the globe, is that Africa does not belong to one nation, but many. If we do not adopt that attitude, we are incomplete.

The investigation done by the detective on my case was not done correctly. The prosecutor interrogated me following the incorrect statement that was given to him by the detective.

One thing that still needs to be revised is the law. We need to emerge with our own legislations, not Roman legislation. When will Africa emerge with constructive logic and aims that touch the globe worldwide? Things mention above need to undergo a re-strategisation concept which will enrich Africa and its people.

May this book
bring you hope,
peace and
purpose to pursue
your goals
that you so richly
deserve.

The VOICE of an
AFRICAN MAN
calling in the midst of nowhere